If Two Shall Agree

The Story of Paul A. Rader
and Kay F. Rader
of The Salvation Army

Carroll Ferguson Hunt

Beacon Hill Press of Kansas City
Kansas City, Missouri

Copyright 2001
by Beacon Hill Press of Kansas City

ISBN 083-411-9285

Printed in the
United States of America

Cover Design: Michael Walsh

Crest Books and Carroll Ferguson Hunt are pleased to provide *If Two Shall Agree: The Story of Paul A. Rader and Kay F. Rader of The Salvation Army* to Beacon Hill Press of Kansas City. We pray that the publisher's ministry, combined with that of The Salvation Army, will be strengthened by the message of this book. Crest Books is the publishing imprint of The Salvation Army National Headquarters, 615 Slaters Lane, Alexandria, Virginia.

Library of Congress Cataloging-in-Publication Data

Hunt, Carroll Ferguson.
    If two shall agree : the story of General Paul A. Rader and Commissioner Kay F. Rader of the Salvation Army / Carroll Ferguson Hunt.
        p. cm.
    ISBN 0-8341-1928-5 (pbk.)
    1. Salvation Army—Biography. 2. Rader, Paul A. (Paul Alexander), 1934- 3. Rader, Kay F. (Kay Frances), 1935- I. Title.

BX9741 .H86 2001
287.9'5'0922—dc21
[B]   2001043575

10   9   8   7   6   5   4   3   2   1

Contents

General Paul A. Rader and Commissioner Kay F. Rader

Foreword

YOU ARE ABOUT TO READ an exhilarating biography about two very exceptional disciples of Jesus Christ. I am privileged to count General Paul and Commissioner Kay Rader as cherished friends and as two among the most influential leaders of contemporary Christianity.

The consistent intimacy of Paul and Kay's prayer life and the integrity of their characters have led to an impelling intentionality of discipleship that is dynamic. Over the years I have been deeply impressed with the verve and vitality of their leadership. I have never visited with them without sensing an impelling vision for the next step of Christ's strategy for them personally, for their leadership in The Salvation Army, and for the world. Here are two followers of the Master who have pulled out all the stops, not only in their own commitment to the Savior but also for the limitless opportunities to expand the evangelization of the world and for the impact on the spiritual and social needs of people. Long before they were elevated to the highest offices of the Army, they were global visionaries with an indefatigable, indomitable viability. They are so much more than "can do" enthusiasts; they are "Christ is able" enablers.

If I'm carrying coals to New Castle in the foreword, be sure of this: they are live, red-hot, flaming coals. I'm a great admirer of The Salvation Army and have worked closely with its offices and members in each phase of my ministry. I've led retreats for its officers and spoken at its conventions. There's a drumbeat within the Army that's more than the beat of the drums of its bands; it is the drumbeat of the Master setting the cadences of global mission. There is a restlessness that presses the movement forward to new frontiers of reaching in the world for Christ. The reverberations of that drumbeat are palpable at any gathering of the Army. Paul and Kay Rader exemplify two lives responsive to that drumbeat.

In this book you will sense the vital role of the families that nurtured these two exceptional leaders. As you read, you will feel the influence of Kay and Paul's parents. The account of the Rader family depicts the solidarity and oneness of an Army family, and Kay's family reveals the impact of their conversion and commitment to Christ and the quality of character that resulted.

The story line of God's grace and guidance in bringing Paul and Kay together at Asbury College and on through the beginning and growth of their ministry is impelling. It leads you through the joy and challenges of obedience to Christ.

This book is rich devotional reading as well. You will find your own life enriched by the honest reporting of how these two faced difficulties, what they learned in times of sickness, and how they faced and conquered adversity. There is a "you are there" authenticity that makes the reader more than an aloof observer of two now world-renowned leaders.

The fabric of the leadership of Paul and Kay Rader exposes the strong threads of both of them woven together inseparably. This book provides a close look at that fabric. It reveals the unique contribution of each of them and yet the intertwining of their interdependence and most of all their total dependence on the Lord.

Paul Rader's indelible mark on The Salvation Army's history is his courageous redefinition of the possible. He is committed to the Lord of the impossible. His career is distinguished by this desire to discover where the Lord is moving and join Him. I admire his thorough training as an Army officer and his insatiable hunger and thirst for fresh insight and knowledge. He is a first-rate scholar as well as a knowledgeable missionary strategist, compelling evangelist, and church growth expert.

It was a special delight in 2000 to be one of the speakers at the Army's International Millennial Congress in Atlanta and to see the fulfillment of General Rader's call for a million soldiers marching into the new millennium "wholly committed to Christ and the Colors." He challenged, "With 800,000 senior soldiers, The Salvation Army is a powerful instrument in the hand of God for world evangelization. . . . Our hurting world needs the Army in strength! The goal of a million senior officers can and must be achieved, but not without focused, prayer-powered, creatively strategized and energetically pursued effort in every territory and command in the world." No wonder the vision was realized. "Lift up Jesus, high over all! Then we will be ready for the 21st century and beyond," the General said in a sermon.

Kay Rader, as you will see in this book, is not only an example of "partnership in mission" but also a lodestar leader in her own right. In a very positive, winsome way she pressed on to the realization of Catherine Booth's vision for women officers, and the implementation of the 10 recommendations for the 1994 Commission on Ministry of Women. Kay and Paul work as a team in prayer and shared responsibilities in a way that maximizes the gifts of both of them. Kay really believes that you can't win a war with half an army and works for the utilization of women officers. Undergirding her work as the Army's World President of Women's Organizations was Commissioner Kay's conviction: "Evangeline Booth said that women were treading new paths and lighting new lamps. We live in a time when this is true around the world. Catherine Booth was a great believer in women taking their place alongside men as preachers and evangelists. I would like to be remembered as one who had tried to keep the dream of Catherine Booth alive for women officers in The Salvation Army." She accomplished her goal on the platform, in high-level conferences, and on the far-flung reaches of missionary outposts in the midst of human misery and anguish.

In my office is a statuette of William Booth. When I look at it, often I think of how Paul and Kay Rader emulate General Booth's statement of commitment in a 20th- and now 21st-century way. "I will tell you the secret," said Booth. "God has had all that there was of me. There have been men with greater brains than I, even greater opportunities, but from the day I got the poor of London on my heart and caught a vision of what Jesus Christ could do with me and them, on that day I made up my mind that God should have all of William Booth that there was. And if there is anything of power in The Salvation Army, it is because God has had all the adoration of my heart, all the power of my will, and all the influence of my life."

When you finish reading this excellent biography of Paul and Kay Rader, you will agree that the secret of their greatness has been that God has had all that there is of them, replenished with supernatural power of the Lord.

—Lloyd J. Ogilvie
Chaplain, U.S. Senate

Prologue

WHEN LIEUTENANT COLONEL ROYSTON BARTLETT tapped on the doors, General Paul and Commissioner Kay Rader exited their London offices and moved together toward the stairs. Tall, silver-haired, and faultlessly dressed in Salvation Army uniforms, they exchanged a momentary glance, one that carried experience, mutual respect, and acknowledgment that one of life's turning points was upon them.

Both Raders moved briskly down the stairs toward Bramwell Booth Hall on the lowest level of the Salvation Army's International Headquarters at 101 Queen Victoria Street, between Saint Paul's Cathedral and the Thames River. The General talked with other officers who fell in beside him, while Commissioner Kay walked with Royston, the General's aide-de-camp and friend to them both.

Kay murmured to Royston "I've got a sharp pain in my middle."

"I can understand that," he responded.

"Lord, help me," Kay prayed silently.

Kay was suffering from apprehension and misgivings about the upcoming ceremony. The Rader generalship was at an end, and on this July day in London they had but one final task to fulfill. She worried about that task, about the kind of reaction they might foment with yet another break with tradition. Would the disapprovers blame her? After all, ever since the days of Adam and Eve, those perceived as pushy women have been cited as culprits for everything from disobeying God to curdling the milk.

Nearing the hall, they could hear music. An ensemble from the Army's International Staff Band was playing, creating an upbeat, festive feeling, and the buzz of many voices let them know the auditorium was filled with expectant people. Headquarters officers and employees plus a number of people from the National Headquarters of the United Kingdom gathered for the unveiling of the portrait of General Paul Alexander Rader, first United

States-born General of The Salvation Army, who was now retiring after five years in office.

This unveiling of generals' portraits is an Army tradition of long standing, and a procession of oil paintings marches around the perimeter of the auditorium. Generals standing and sitting, holding Bibles, flanked with flags, one even with a coat over his arm, all solemn and wise and purposeful, all known, remembered, revered. There were 14 of them from founder William Booth to Rader's predecessor, Canadian Bramwell Tillsley.

And now on an easel to the left of the platform and veiled by the red, blue and gold of the Salvation Army flag stood another portrait ready to take its place on the walls with the others.

The Commissioner and the General entered the hall and took seats on the platform facing the crowd. The General felt calm, free from anxiety as his fingers sought again in his pocket the notes that outlined his remarks to be made before the unveiling.

Commissioner Kay, on the other hand, confronted the plague of butterflies within as her gaze swept the murmuring crowd, gauging their mood and spirit. Both Raders, after all, were no strangers to innovation, to change, to challenging tradition in the face of protest and disagreement. This moment was no exception, for prodded, they knew, by the Holy Spirit, they were again sidestepping tradition in pursuit of what they felt persuaded was the greater good. So some questions awaited resolution; Commissioner Kay knew this well as her eyes moved across the auditorium.

How would this crowd of fellow officers—coworkers, critics, and friends—react to this final gesture of their leadership?

Kay found encouragement in the smiles she encountered as she scanned the crowd. Even a couple of thumbs-up signals flashed her way, which helped to soothe the pain that attacked her on the way down the stairs.

General Rader rose to speak. He told the waiting crowd that they were about to see not an oil painting, but a photograph, a departure from more than 100 years of tradition. He explained that as other generals symbolized their leadership by what appeared with them in their portraits, the same was true for him.

"After all we did together, it would be inappropriate for me to appear alone." With this comment he signaled what everyone was about to see.

Both Raders moved off the platform and walked to the easel where the portrait stood, still covered and invisible. Time for the unveiling. Five years of leadership at an end. The generalship of The Salvation Army and the World Presidency of Women's Organizations were being handed into other, already designated, hands. Paul and Kay Rader were leaving their leadership of The Salvation Army with the imprint of what they, before God, believed to be major priorities for the 21st century.

Paul pulled the cord, and the flag slid off to the side, revealing the General and the Commissioner pictured together before a global map of the world that filled the portrait edge to edge.

It was not an oil painting, but a digitally produced photograph; not a portrait of the General alone, but of husband and wife together, a pair of partners, against the backdrop of God's beloved waiting world, reinforcing the underlying motif of their leadership. "We are partners in mission; coworkers under God." The message of the portrait, then, is global mission. Coupled with that, as in the Raders' lives and ministry, is partnership, emphasizing the role of women equal with men in responsibility to take the gospel to the world.

Created by Nick Clark, one of London's most prominent photographers, the portrait shows both the Commissioner and the General before the world to which they dedicated themselves in answer to God's call to each of them individually more than 40 years before.

But why partnership? Doesn't everybody already know that of course wives and husbands in Christian ministry work together? What are the practical and spiritual ramifications of this term? What is so different here from what already goes on in The Salvation Army, or in other denominations and Christian agencies, for that matter? Why partnership?

"You can't run an army on half its soldiers." That's why.

Both Raders—through 25 years of both training and experience within The Salvation Army—developed the belief that men and women on every ministry team should share equally in the opportunities and responsibilities confronting that team wherever in the world it was assigned. Too often, they learned, women, called by God as were the men, rode the pack mules into battle, although they were as equipped and trained and capable as the front-line special forces to whose ranks they were denied admission.

The Army has as one of its oldest traditions, originated by founders Catherine and William Booth, that God expects His called ones, women and men, to preach, to serve, to nurture, to rescue without respect to the gender of the rescuer or the preacher, nor in deference to whatever cultural prejudices might impinge on strategy choices.

As missionaries in Korea right out of officer training, the Raders began to discover their conviction that wives and husbands as Army officers must work together as equals. Added to that was General Rader's conviction, built upon 30-plus years of study and experience, that partnership with other members of the Christian community enhances and strengthens the social aid and evangelistic efforts of each participant. The practical ramifications of these convictions transferred, in part, from Asia to the West as their assignments shifted and their responsibilities increased—from New York to Pennsylvania to California, wherever their assignments took them; from officer training to welfare project supervision, from evangelism to rehabilitation, responsibilities for divisions and territories, people and projects.

"You can't run an army on half its soldiers." Commissioner Kay said it, and they both believe it without equivocation, so they modeled partnership through shared preaching duties, through equally responsible assignments. Neither rode the other's coattails. They strode together through their work and their days, modeling principles upon which The Salvation Army was begun a century and a half before. And whenever it proved appropriate, General Rader, as he had done since student days, sought cooperation, shared expertise, and participated with other Evangelical organizations in spiritual cross-pollenization of the things of God.

Looking back across the years and examining the roots, the beginnings, and the formation of Paul Rader and Kay Fuller, one can spot some sprouting seeds of promise, a few twigs bent toward the light that suggest what was to come.

1
Destined to Be Different

IN THE GLARING LIGHT preferred by their Dad, five young heads bent over black-bound Bibles open before them on the dining room table. Before each child also sat a small block of wood drilled with five holes in which stood five colored Scripto pencils, straight up and ready for action. Red represented salvation, blue was for holiness, yellow was for prophecy, green was for promises, and black was for judgment.

The mother of this brood of children sat silently at the foot of the table, her eyes on her own Bible while the father with a voice like a trumpet read from his.

"'But God commendeth his love toward us, in that, while we were yet sinners, Christ died for us.'

"That's Rom. 5:8, children. Do you have it? Gladdie, make sure the little guys find the place. Now—what color should we mark this with? Who knows? Damon? Jeanne?"

A couple of young children, showing promise of vocal strength to match their father's, announced, "Red! It's salvation!"

Family prayers in the Rader household at 179 Renner Avenue, Newark, New Jersey, were never quick and cursory—not simply a verse, a prayer, and out the door. After supper each night out came the King James Bibles, the blocks of wood—cut, sanded, drilled, and varnished by the man at the head of the table—and the colored Scripto pencils, which may have cost only 25 cents each but were no small investment on a Salvation Army Captain's pay with a family of five children. The Rader parents seemed to think it worth the outlay. Intense discussion usually characterized their meal times, conversations about scripture and books, plus instruction from Dad on how to share one's faith.

They called it a conspiracy of love, for they intended that their children would each find salvation and a place of ministry in the name of Christ, so they left nothing to chance.

Paul Alexander Rader, middle child of the five born to Lyell Mayes and Gladys Mina Damon Rader, was born on 15th Street in Manhattan March 14, 1934. Although the family lived in the Bronx at the time, Gladys went to the Salvation Army's Booth Memorial Hospital for Paul's arrival.

Paul's first name came from Paul O. Rader, his father's brother and a young Salvation Army officer who, poised and ready for missionary service in India, had been killed by lightning at Camp Wonderland near Boston as he struggled to get camper children in his care out of a lake to safety during a sudden storm. That Paul, in turn, had been named for evangelist Paul Rader, who pastored Moody Memorial Church in Chicago, led the Christian and Missionary Alliance for a time, and spearheaded the tabernacle movement in the 1920s. Alexander, Paul's middle name, came from his maternal grandfather, Alexander M. Damon, first American-born Territorial Commander in The Salvation Army. He bore the rank of Commissioner and was a close associate of General Evangeline Booth.

Younger brother to Jeanne and Damon and preceding Herbert and Lyell III, Paul grew into a typical city boy in some ways, playing stickball on the streets. He hungered after toy guns like those the neighbor boys played with, but his mother, Gladys, of pacifistic Quaker stock on her mother's side, forbade them. So while Paul cast envious eyes at the other kids with their cap pistols holstered low on their hips, the best he could do was carry in his hand a broken stick for which he had to provide the noise— and worry lest his mother catch him at that.

Cutting out paper soldiers and arranging them in ranks, another boyhood pleasure, plunged Paul into serious trouble, for while searching the attic for paper with which to make his soldiers, he came up with an old scrapbook of his father's. Here he found sheets and sheets of good white paper printed on only one side, so the boy made his soldiers. When he showed them off that evening to his parents, he learned that he had destroyed copies of a series of articles his father had written during a journey through the Holy Land. For that misstep, Paul received a spanking he never forgot. Paul's father could mete out swift, harsh punishment upon his children, and Paul sometimes caught the brunt of his displeasure.

But spankings notwithstanding, Lyell Rader believed in a conspiracy of love and in using such a conspiracy on his children to train them for service. He brought not only Bibles and colored pencils to bear on their thinking each day, but as an engineer and an amateur scientist, he created object lessons that leaned heavily toward chemicals, physics, and natural phenomena like snake venom and light refraction off hummingbird feathers.

Paul's father, Lyell Mayes Rader Jr., emerged from a crop of remarkable Raders who for over a century hurled their hearts, their energies, their superb intellects, and their strong voices into the battle to win souls for God.

Lyell Jr. used his prodigious knowledge of things mechanical and chemical to communicate the gospel's good news, but never in a prosaic or predictable manner. While stationed at the "Glory Shop," the Salvation Army storefront mission 50 feet from Broadway in New York's Times Square, his unique forays into the streets called for a "gospel chariot." It was a portable booth decked out in flags and Salvation Army advertising and topped with a beach umbrella, from which he performed chemistry lessons that pointed his hearers to God.

Never one to fit into the common mold, the majority of Lyell Rader's Salvation Army assignments had to do with territorial revivalism and divisional youth work. His children spoke of his absences in Army jargon as Dad being "out specialing."

Damon, two years older than Paul, was in many ways his father's alter ego, as strongly interested in science and electronics as his parent. He later acquired a master of science degree from Carnegie Tech University before officer training. But Paul? No. Try as he might to care about the paraphernalia and what it produced, he much preferred to cut out his soldiers and line them up in rows or to play table games with Jeanne, with whom he shared a warm and abiding relationship. He loved art, music, and books, and, fortunately for him, both parents encouraged these interests without prejudice against his tastes. He did try, though, to measure up to his father's expectations, for the time came when Lyell Rader tried to teach his children to do as he did. Paul one fateful night was assigned to perform a simple experiment, one of his dad's object lessons during an open-air meeting on a New England sidewalk.

All that remains of that fiasco in Paul's memory is the fact that at the appropriate moment in his talk, flames were supposed to shoot out from under his foot, but all his efforts produced was a miserable wisp of smoke. So while waiting and hoping for a miracle, Paul ranted on for a bit about the fire power of the Holy Spirit or some such predictable dogma, all the time peering down at the unignited experiment and wishing the sidewalk would please open up and swallow him.

"I learned something about spiritual gifts that night," he remembers. "My father's experiments were certainly not my gift. That was clear."

But Paul loved everything he was learning about The Salvation Army as he grew. One of his earliest memories as a very small boy is of sitting on a radiator at the Times Square Corps and singing with everyone else "This one thing I know. . . ." He loved going to corps and was thrilled beyond words over his first uniform, which he acquired by joining a young people's singing company. After all, The Salvation Army was his heritage, passed on to him and his siblings by both mother and father. Even before Raders came into the Army, aggressive evangelism marked almost everything Paul's ancestors did.

Although guesswork characterizes most genealogical sleuthwork, it is sure that Raders appeared in the United States early in the 18th century. A number of Paul's forebears fought in the American Revolution. It is also sure that Paul Alexander Rader's branch of the family tree headed West, leaving traces of their influence in churches and courthouses, schools, ranches, and settlements along the way.

Paul's grandfather, Lyell Sr., was the elder brother of Paul Rader, one of America's most prominent and innovative evangelists during the Jazz Age of the 1920s, a familiar name in evangelical circles and the subject of much study. Lyell Sr. was an industrial chemist involved in the development of several well-known products and processes early in the 20th century.

A man huge of voice and bulk—one of his relatives remembered him loving his food almost as much as he loved his Savior—after turning his life over to God, he became an advocate for Christianity whom people must have found impossible to ignore. When they could get away with it, Paul and his siblings called him "big fat Grandpa" behind his back, not too surprising since the man stood over six feet tall, weighed more than 350 pounds, and could make himself heard over a brass band's best crescendo. No amount of reprimands and disapproval could stamp out the children's name for their remarkable grandfather.

As a boy in Wyoming, Grandpa Rader claimed, on ranches where he sought work, the horses turned and ran when they saw him coming. He did better at Denver University, where the football team welcomed him with open arms.

Grandpa Rader died of a stroke in 1938, cutting off the possibility of a longer relationship with his grandchildren, whose contact with him was all too brief. The Rader five, on the other hand, knew their Damon grandparents well, and from them and from their mother they absorbed what it meant to have Salvation Army traditions dominate every aspect of their lives.

Gladys Rader, gentle and soft-spoken mother to her brood, was the daughter of Alexander Damon and of Annie Barrow Damon, who was born to English Quakers. Commissioned to Salvation Army officership before her marriage to Lyell Rader Jr., she left a notebook full of handwritten Bible studies, usually thematic, and a few sayings and quotes she must have thought significant—but all without personal observations. Included in that notebook are pages of verses under the heading "Verses for Children's Letters." As her five children eventually scattered across the world—to India, Africa, Sri Lanka, Korea—whenever she wrote them, she included a bit of the Word chosen just for them.

On occasion Paul's father would say to his children, "God has been with this family for a long time. He's been at work placing His people, so God is at work preparing you to fit into this picture somewhere."

Paul listened to his father's words and absorbed the responsibility, responding within himself with intensity typical of youth. He spent time with the Lord and studied His Word. He plunged into the intense discussions over family meals led by his father, or his mother in her turn whenever Dad was absent.

Some children struggle against any threat of difference between them and their peer group, often rebelling against parental edicts that fail to conform to what's going on among their friends. Remarkably, Paul did not feel this with his friends at school and attributes it in part to the fact that he attended class with many Jewish students for whom religious dictates were a way of life.

"Yeah, well, I don't go to movies. You see . . ." he might feel forced to explain.

"No movies? Really? What . . . is it a religious thing?"

"Yeah, kinda."

"Oh, well then. We're religious, too, you know. We don't eat pork."

No pressure there.

Paul did encounter another sort of pressure at school, however. Math courses were a challenge. But he studied extra hard and managed to get through them. English and Latin were more to his liking, although making top grades in any subject was not on his list of achievements for most of his public school years.

Paul also found it difficult to be aggressive in evangelism, an expectation that weighed on his mind as he stood in the shadow of his strong, domineering evangelist father who always, always had a word of exhortation for everyone. Lyell talked to persons in the tollbooths at the bridges and tunnels leading in and out of New York. He buttonholed the neighbor in the apartment elevator heading down with his garbage. Being a silent observer to these witnessing moments by his father often made young Paul cringe with embarrassment.

Determined to rise above this reticence, however, as a teenager Salvationist Paul spoke freely in front of shabby Newark saloons about his commitment to follow Jesus. And he loved going to the corps, even though in the Newark-New York days that meant almost every night. He sat down in front so nothing could interfere with his absorption of what was going on. Again remarkably, when invitation time came, Paul would talk to people in the congregation, both at the corps and during open-air meetings, to individuals he thought might be weighing the possibility of praying at the mercy seat. But his approach was oblique, never blunt nor direct.

"Hello, how are you tonight?"

"I'm OK."

"Good. What did you think of the speaker?"

"Uh, she did OK."

"What about what she said? What did you think of that?"

Paul and his brothers regarded it a special privilege to be sons of Salvation Army officers involved in youth work. Famous for their summer camps, the Army maintained a camp for boys in Butler, New Jersey, in the Ramapo Mountains, and the Rader boys left the city and hiked off to Tecumseh Village at Star Lake to spend their summers. Captain Henry Berkhoudt and his wife, Phyllis, directed the camp, exerting a strong, lasting influence on Paul Rader. At Berkhoudt's camp he made public his commitment to Jesus Christ as Savior and Lord of his life. He remembers clearly that Sunday evening at the lakeside campfire amphitheater when he tearfully opened his heart to the Savior. According to an article written by Margaret Troutt for *Power for Teens,* published by Scripture Press Foundation, Paul said that until he was 12 years old he "considered his Christian conduct 'a matter of convenience and conformity,'" but that night "he recognized himself as a sinner. . . . 'I knew I needed to be born again.'" He acknowledged that he "'didn't find it easy to kneel before my buddies at a crude plank set on cement blocks, but I finally did it.'"

Lyell Rader carried yet another round of ammunition in his arsenal of ways to build into his children the precepts and doctrines of the Christian way, and more, of the best methods of living and serving the Lord and helping to build His kingdom.

"I'll buy you any book you'll read," he pledged. "This way you'll build a good library for when you go off to college."

By this time no doubt lingered in the Rader children's minds that Dad did not mean comic books or best-selling novels—nothing of the sort. On the recommended reading list were Hannah Whitehall Smith's *The Christian's Secret of a Happy Life,* Norman Grubb's *Touching the Invisible,* Wilbur Smith's *Therefore Stand,* and others by Paget Wilkes, J. Sidlow Baxter, and of course, Commissioner Samuel Brengle, beginning with *Helps to Holiness.* Paul went off to college eventually with 20 or 30 such demanding tomes competing for shelf space with his textbooks.

Gladys and Lyell Rader were passionately committed to the salvation of their children, first and foremost. They bore a strategy in mind that they followed with discipline and great care. They spoke often of their own joy in service and of ministry as a vital part of their children's lives in the future. Paul grew to feel that this was inevitable.

At times it seems as if every officer in The Salvation Army and most of the soldiers play brass instruments. Music marked the methods of the Army from its founding in the 19th century in England as did public marches, so brass bands have set the pace for much of what the Army does since the beginning. And the Rader kids joined the procession in their turn.

Paul loved music, and when the business of lessons came up, the first arbitrary choice of instrument handed him an alto horn. When that proved to be a poor choice, Paul's father soon made a change for him—to trombone. It wasn't long until Paul won the division's soloist contest at music camp. He polished his skills with some of the finest teachers available. Erik Leidzen was one of these. Swedish born, he was widely regarded as America's most eminent composer and arranger for brass bands. Paul always felt that Leidzen was larger than life—"one only meets a few such persons in a lifetime." This maestro shaped the boy's views forever as regards excellence. "Music must express the depth and integrity of your devotion to Christ," Leidzen said. "Let it express your spiritual sensitivity."

Leidzen often appeared at the music camps where Paul

trained and learned. Their paths crossed again during Paul's time
at the Army's officer training college, and as their teacher-pupil
relationship strengthened, Paul was often privileged to play under
Leidzen's baton.

As his musical gifts flowered, he worked with some of the
best brass instrumentalists around, including Robert Lambert at
the Curtis Institute in Philadelphia, trombonist in the renowned
Philadelphia Orchestra under the direction of Eugene Ormandy.

"Sometimes we'd get to a concert at the Academy of Music
and sit up under the rafters in the cheap seats. I'd peer way down
to the stage and see my teacher there. What a thrill!"

Later on, Lyell and Gladys Rader were appointed to new responsibilities at divisional headquarters in Cincinnati. Jeanne and
Damon were already attending Asbury College, about 100 miles
away in Kentucky. During Paul's last year in high school and
while at Asbury College himself, he also studied at the Cincinnati
Conservatory of Music with former Salvationist professor Ernest
Glover, principal trombonist with the Cincinnati Symphony Orchestra, and played in one of his renowned brass ensembles.

Another benefit emerged for Paul from the move to Ohio. His
intensive involvement in the whirl of activities at corps and
school evaporated, which meant that time for academic activities
expanded. Paul's grades in this last year of high school jumped
from low B's to A's, which made college entrance no hurdle
whatsoever.

Meanwhile, the probable source of Paul's penchant for art,
good music, and well-turned phrases—his mother—also provided both inspiration and discipline for her middle child along with
the other four, each one strong and talented and individualistic.
Gladys Rader usually faded into the background in the presence
of her husband, for he seized the spotlight—perhaps automatically, even unwittingly—on every stage he ever mounted. One of
her young grandchildren, Edie, elder daughter of Kay and Paul
and already astute, commented, "Nana does a lot of listening,
doesn't she?"

Gladys was very bright and an effective officer before her
marriage to Lyell Rader, a good communicator in her teaching

and preaching. But in the years following their wedding, she had little opportunity to use her gifts, especially in public ministry. Her husband was the headliner. If this ever troubled her, she never let on. Instead, she imbued her children with love for the Lord and The Salvation Army both by her example, which revealed her values, and also by conversation and devotions around the table in the absence of her husband, who was frequently on the road. At those moments Nana did the talking, and her rowdy, talkative brood listened carefully.

Gladys was not afraid to tackle the hard parts when it came to disciplining her children. Paul displeased her once, and in an effort to show her young son how sin affects our fellowship with God, she calmly told him, "You've broken fellowship with me." She withdrew from the normal chatter and laughter of their relationship, crushing the boy's heart and impressing on him for all time the seriousness of sin and its consequences in separating us from intimate fellowship with God.

Coupled with Gladys Rader's courage in disciplining her children were limitless love and spiritual discernment that marked her children for life. She prayed over each one as he or she left for school every morning. Paul felt the touch of her hand on his head forever afterward and heard her words: "Remember who you are."

The memories of his mother's place in the shadows in spite of her training, experience, and abilities that would have, could have, shone widely across the world planted in Paul Rader some seed questions that would eventually affect his views regarding the role of women in ministry.

2

Frances Kay

MOST EVERYBODY IN OCILLA, GEORGIA, knew that Edith and Jimmy Fuller's baby was sick. They had taken her to the hospital, and things didn't look good. Just nine months old, Frances Kay lay like a stone in the white bed, her parents standing by, clenching helpless hands. When the doctor came in to check the baby's pulse, he had nothing to say. They all could see the blue tinge of her eyelids, her tiny fingernails. They all knew what that meant. But none of them knew what to do about it.

The door swung open, and quick footsteps crossed the floor. A woman in a starched white dress with coppery skin and smooth black plaits of hair wrapped round her head pushed past parents and doctor, creating a place for herself at the bedside, remarkable behavior for one such as her. Mariah LaSane stared at the baby for a moment before she spoke.

"Let's talk to the One who knows what he's doin'."

Mariah leaned over the tiny girl and broke into prayer, knowing well what she was doing as she talked to her Savior about rescuing precious Frances Kay, who teetered on the brink of death. The Fullers were not Christian believers, but they bowed their heads as spectators as their hired help addressed the Almighty regarding their baby girl.

After her final firm "Amen," Mariah straightened her back but kept her head bent, eyes fastened on the face on the pillow. As she watched, the child opened her huge hazel eyes and gazed back at Mariah. Her eyelids and fingernails were rosy. The blue was gone. She was healthy, healed.

"I owe my life to her," Kay acknowledges decades later in reflecting on a woman in a starched dress with braids on her head like a crown, a woman who loved her, played with her, taught her about strength and dignity and faithfulness. She was Mariah's precious child, and the security of that knowledge, that bond, gave her the sinews and steady nerves for a lifetime of uncommon demands.

Together they washed turnip greens and did laundry while Mother Edith played bridge or went visiting. While Edith was gone, Mariah sang Christian songs to Frances Kay, songs that in those days the little girl otherwise heard all too seldom.

The Fullers'—and Mariah's—little treasure was born June 2, 1935, three years after her older sister, Mary Jim. The Fullers chose the name of Kay Frances—the Kay because Miss Edith liked it, the Frances for a favorite aunt—but a short time later she discovered a movie star with that name.

"Name your baby for a movie star? Never. That's tookie!" (Farther north, "tookie" would be translated "tacky," but in south Georgia "tookie" said it all.) So they reversed the baby's name, and she became Frances Kay.

Older sister Mary Jim and Frances Kay often played together and formed a closeness that never deserted them. Mary Jim loved the out-of-doors, especially when it included ponies first, and then horses, while Frances Kay's interest turned toward playing with her growing family of dolls. Her daddy built her a playhouse that was the realization of any little girl's dream. Here she could really cook on her little stove and make a home for her dolls. Best of all, Mariah would bend herself into Frances Kay's little house and play with her there for long stretches of time.

Eight years passed before Edith Scott arrived and then six more before the Fullers acquired James Fuller Jr., so Frances Kay and Mary Jim had things pretty much their own way for an idyllic stretch of time. Mr. Jimmy owned and operated a sawmill in Nashville, Georgia, and built a house on the edge of town where his little girls had plenty of room to play. So did the chickens, ducks, cows, pigs, and ponies that came and went.

As Frances Kay grew from a baby into a strong-headed little girl, Mariah didn't allow much discipline of her. In charge of her treasure by now, Mariah grabbed her up and ran if anyone came toward the child with correction in mind. And she could always think of a reason why it wasn't Frances Kay's fault, no matter what had happened.

"If somebody been watchin' her, she wouldn't a done that!" usually worked, especially if woman and child were walking rapidly in the opposite direction.

To add to the mix, Edith Fuller did not relinquish all discipline matters to her husband, as some women might have done. Jimmy Fuller was big, strong, often impulsive, and though his wife was short in stature, she was huge in heart and insisted on having her say when dealing with the girls' misdemeanors. Pampered and protected, she might easily have been spoiled, but Frances Kay knew she had to obey both parents, and this was not hard for her. She was nurtured, surrounded, and sustained by love at every turn and so was usually compliant. She loved her family, each one, dearly, a love fostered in large part by her mother, the baby in a family of 12 children and a former schoolteacher.

"Miss Edith 'loved' learning into her children," was often said of the brown-eyed lady with the gentle smile during her teaching days. And then she was so loving with her girls, as was Mariah, that Frances Kay almost always wanted to please them. Both girls helped at home, and no delineation existed between boys' chores and girls' chores. They chopped the wood, weeded the garden, fed the horses, and helped with the housework. Their father never complained about his lack of sons right up until the time when his was born, and his two older daughters never heard the words "Girls don't do that." The women in Jimmy Fuller's family had always done it all, for they ran stores, pumped gas, and conducted business as competently as any man, so Mary Jim and Frances Kay knew they could handle the challenges they confronted. After all, no one said they couldn't.

The school stood right across the street from the Fuller house, so the girls could listen for the bell to ring, then make their dash and arrive on time.

Frances Kay loved school—everything about it, starting with her first-grade teacher, Olivette Pierce, who lived next door and was "very beautiful." Learning pleased Kay, particularly reading, which she did precociously, occasionally feeling impatient with those who didn't or couldn't read. Reading opened doors to the whole world; how can you *not* read?

The Harrises lived next door to the Fullers on the other side, and their daughter E'Wanna was often playmate of choice for Frances Kay. One fateful day an upstairs room became their beauty shop where in a fit of stylish creativity, each sheared off one side of the other's hair.

Inevitably their mothers discovered their crime, although each dealt with it in a different way. An irate Mrs. Harris spanked E'Wanna thoroughly; Miss Edith laughed, finding the whole episode funny beyond words.

When Mary Jim and Frances Kay were still quite young, the Fuller family often spent those pretelevision evenings before the bedroom fireplace on cool winter evenings. They cracked pecans, made popcorn, and laughed at the funny pictures Mr. Jimmy drew while the girls did their homework. And some significant changes waited just around the corner for the Fuller family that would bless and benefit their lives forever.

Upstanding Southern Americans, Miss Edith and Mr. Jimmy did go to church occasionally, she to the Methodist and he to the Baptist, as they acknowledged their upbringing in separate denominations. Since church was something one did only once in a while to be nice, it didn't matter much one way or the other. But the local Methodist pastor, Brother Roundtree, eventually led Miss Edith to personal faith in Jesus Christ, and life changed significantly in the Fuller house on the edge of town.

Mr. Jimmy watched carefully as his diminutive wife lived out her newly acquired faith. He saw how she stayed home more instead of gallivanting around the county, how she read her Bible, attended her church, taught their girls. He sensed the growing sweetness in her, saw the glow of her joy over a clear conscience and a committed heart. He knew she would obey God no matter what stood in her way.

And he wanted the same thing for himself.

So Jimmy Fuller began with the stuff he knew. A two-pack-a-day man, he abruptly threw away his cigarettes and never smoked again. Down at his sawmill he quit swearing, equally abruptly, and must have collected some stares and whispers from his work-men, for everyone knew he could pollute the air with the most profane of them. In this way a year passed as he watched his wife and tinkered with the symptoms of his unregenerate soul.

Then one summer day a Holiness preacher brought a tent to Nashville, set it up on a vacant lot, and began a series of meet-ings. Brother Fail Andrews' preaching under that canvas tent brought Jimmy Fuller face to face with God, and, hungry for that which his wife displayed so faithfully day after day, he offered to God his strength, his skills, his will, his life.

Mr. Jimmy forever afterward gave Miss Edith the credit for his finding Jesus as Savior. "God brought her to me, and she brought me to God" was his way of summing up their turn to-ward home.

After the Fullers' conversion, the whole family discovered worship at church because the parents, so excited about their newfound faith, plunged into every aspect of how that faith could affect their lives. At Sunday school Frances Kay learned to sing "Praise Him! Praise Him! Jesus, our blessed Redeemer!" and loved it among the best for all time to come.

The cozy times around the fireplace continued but evolved into family worship time marked by Bible reading and conversa-tions about God. As Frances Kay absorbed the excitement ema-nating from her parents over their spiritual transformation, she wanted some, too, so as simply and naturally as drinking cold water to deal with thirst, at her father's knee she invited Jesus to come into her heart.

It wasn't too long until Mr. Jimmy felt God nudging him to do something toward building His kingdom in Nashville. He felt called to preach and wanted to introduce his mill workers to his Savior. So he built the Mill Mission for the people who worked for him, who lived in a ghetto of sorts and—White or Black—were not welcome in other Nashville places of worship. These were unwashed, unlearned, unaccepted people, and Mr. Jimmy wanted to help them toward the light.

And it worked. The mill workers were the first ones to attend the little mission where they got saved, after which they began to clean up and work toward economic stability. Country folk, share croppers, and small landowners also heard about the little church for people like them, so they harnessed up the mule, boosted the kids into the back of the wagon, and drove to the edge of Nashville, Georgia, on Sunday mornings.

Miss Edith, Mary Jim, Frances Kay, baby Edith Scott, and Mr. Jimmy were always there, too.

Jimmy Fuller came by his social concern and his kindly impulses honestly. His paternal great-grandfather was a Baptist preacher in Georgia and one of the first to give land to freed slaves. Fullers have been in the United States since the beginning, for there were Fullers among the pilgrims on the Mayflower. The Fullers came from Scotland and England, as did the Raders, but that name wouldn't matter to Frances Kay for some time yet.

Meanwhile she took piano lessons beginning in the second grade. Miss Paxson was the school music teacher, and Frances Kay loved the specialness of getting out of class and "prissing down the hall," as she puts it, for her weekly lesson. Miss Paxson wore lots of lipstick, it seems, and thought Frances Kay was a wonderful pianist surely destined for a concert career.

Then the Fullers' little girl graduated from the teacher offered by the Nashville grade school and took lessons from Mrs. Scruggs at her house. Contrary to the inclination of most children, Frances Kay enjoyed practicing, and her lessons continued through the eighth grade, when the Fuller family moved to Fort Valley, Georgia. She lost her teacher and never took lessons again, a lifelong source of regret.

One of the pronouncements Frances Kay heard from her father's lips affected her far more dramatically than the discontinued piano lessons, however. Mr. Jimmy used to say of his life before conversion, "Sometimes I felt lost, but I thought nobody was looking for me."

This statement affected Frances Kay as a child and as a woman. In adulthood she often reflected on the popular Evangelical teaching that God speaks to wives and families only through the head of the house, the male. But she saw how the Lord used her mother to draw

Jimmy Fuller to himself, and she heard him affirm this over and over again. God chose Edith as His representative to reach the burly businessman. Frances Kay knew this through all her growing-up years. She also knew that her mother didn't sit around waiting for her husband to make the first move. After all, Miss Edith, although a southern lady with soft voice and gentle manners, was the former Miss Edith Strother from English Northumberland stock, which means strong, very strong. She prayed for him and talked to him about the wonders of redemption even as she lived before him a Christ-filled life, stimulating in her husband a spiritual hunger as he recognized that in his lostness someone was seeking him after all.

As the Fuller parents progressed in their spiritual pilgrimage and strengthening marriage, their obvious commitment to each other stabilized and strengthened their four children, teaching the girls that they were not hampered by their gender. They were people, just like everyone else.

After the Fuller conversion to Christian living, Mr. Jimmy began inviting hordes of traveling preachers to enjoy the hospitality of his home. His children found the company always intriguing but at times frustrating as well. Frances Kay squirmed under the edict that children, beloved treasures though they be, should keep quiet and listen to the grownups talk. She held opinions about things, though, things she wanted to say. And being well-schooled by Miss Edith in fine table manners, she found the behavior of some of the visiting preachers beyond belief. Like the one who combined his enjoyment of Mariah's fried chicken with his love of talking with his mouth full.

"You look like you have a tractor in your mouth," she informed the garrulous evangelist. Not the best moment in the annals of Fuller hospitality.

Another high point in family history was when Frances Kay showed up at the breakfast table with her sunglasses on. This time the visiting preachers stopped their chewing and chuckled over the little girl's outrageous behavior—but Miss Edith was not amused. Knowing precisely what her second child was trying to pull, swift and accurate came her order: "Frances Kay, you march yourself back upstairs and wash your face!"

In retrospect, Kay admits to being disturbed by some of the new post-conversion dimensions to their family life. She resented their visitors' intrusive egos, their dominance of all conversations, and at times their hellfire-and-brimstone antics.

Plus, they ate too much of the food.

Jimmy Fuller noticed this as well as he pointed out to Mariah one day while bringing her to work.

"Well, Mariah, we had a biblical incident at our house last night."

"What was that, Mr. Jimmy?"

"Pharoah's army came—that's what."

As Kay remembers it, they *always* had Pharoah's army at the Fuller house.

Jimmy Fuller felt that the Lord would have him join his evangelist friends on the road, preaching wherever opportunities arose and helping others to find peace at the Cross. The Mill Mission was thriving, so he sold his sawmill and moved his family a little ways north to Fort Valley, Georgia. Mary Jim was off to college, Miss Edith was occupied with Edith Scott and baby Jimbo, and as Mr. Jimmy disappeared down the road to his revival meetings, it fell to 14-year-old Frances Kay to learn to drive the car and help keep the family functioning, a part of her education that affected how she would and could handle responsibility in the years to come.

3

What's a Salvationist?

SOMEWHERE ALONG ABOUT NINTH GRADE, when the Fuller family moved to Fort Valley, Georgia, and Mr. Jimmy launched his career in itinerant evangelism, Frances Kay lost half her name. As she entered high school in this new town, her fellow teenagers said, "Oh, no—you can't be 'Frances Kay.' We're just gonna call you 'Kay.'" And Kay she is, to family, friends and her worldwide collection of acquaintances and coworkers.

"Kay Fuller" was what Paul Rader was told when he inquired about her of a fellow student at Asbury College in Wilmore, Kentucky. Paul was standing in line at the cafeteria when he looked across the room above the heads of hundreds of chattering students and saw an "exceedingly attractive" girl at the ice cream dispenser. Her bearing and confident aura caught his eye. Tall, slim, and brown-haired, she stood out from the crowd and made him want to know more.

Paul planted himself on the library steps, a way station of sorts then, the best place on campus to see and be seen, for everyone passed by there on their trek to classes, dorms, conferences, or trysts. The first Artist Series (formal-dress concerts by visiting performers) was coming up, and he determined to persuade Kay to be his date. Eventually she passed by the library. He asked her out, and she accepted.

Paul was a sophomore at Asbury. Jeanne and Damon were there, too, and the Rader name was well known, thanks to the academic skills, musical talent, and leadership potential of the three. Maintaining three children in college is an unsettling prospect even for the most affluent, but for a Salvation Army officer, even one as creative as Lyell Rader, such an assignment approaches the impossible. Lyell's cousin, Bernice Cory, was editor-in-chief at Scripture Press, which she and her husband, Victor, founded and saw develop into one of the giants of the Christian publishing world. Raders and Corys were close, and when the time came for college for each of Lyell and Gladys Rader's five children, Aunt Bace (pronounced "Basie") saw to it that sufficient funds became available to cover the cost. The same God who provided bread in the desert for thousands of His chosen people guaranteed that five remarkable individuals would receive their training for worldwide service in His name.

Paul commuted back to Cincinnati frequently for trombone lessons with Professor Ernest Glover at the conservatory, but contrary to his earlier pattern as a freshman, he did not go so regularly to the corps there because he had joined an evangelism team made up of student evangelist Jim DiRaddo, a girls' trio who called themselves the King's Karolers (members were Phyllis Thomas, Carolyn Reeder and Carroll Ferguson), and pianist Barbara McGilvray. This group traveled throughout the region on weekends, and Paul's music leadership and trombone solo work enhanced their evangelistic services significantly, not to mention the strong contribution of his Salvationist fervor dedicated to seeing sinners born again.

Shortly after he nailed his Artist Series date with Kay, Paul had a free weekend and invited her out for dinner on campus so they could get to know each other. Each of them carries the memory of that evening as filled with hours and hours of talk. Paul had a sense that "this is someone I want to know."

"We had no awkward silences where we couldn't think of anything to say," Kay remembers. "It was comfortable." All very intriguing, Paul found it, and he determined to keep it going from there.

Some natural barriers loomed between this Army lad—a son of the regiment—born and raised in New York, and the south Georgia girl who had never even heard of a Salvationist.

When Kay arrived at Asbury College, one of the first people

she noticed was a small, beautiful girl with dark, curly hair and a smile that could light any room.

"Who's that?" Kay asked her roommate, Betty Teece.

"She's June Dearin, a Salvationist."

"What's a Salvationist?" Not only was Kay learning about her new college environment, but she was running up against terms, such as Salvationist, which she had never encountered back home. Betty's answer was simple. "Someone who belongs to The Salvation Army."

One Saturday night at a college sing Kay also noticed, before he asked her for a date, Paul Rader leading the music and playing a trombone with remarkable skill.

"Who's that?" she wanted to know.

Her roommate again provided the information: "That's Paul, Damon Rader's brother."

This intimidated the 18-year-old freshman because she had observed the dynamic, always-in-a-hurry Damon riding his bicycle across campus toward class, and she knew he was student body president. Something about his high-energy, high-visibility, Eastern seaboard persona scared her just a bit.

On the other hand, Damon's younger brother was a different story. She liked what she saw at the college sing. His music, his public presence, his purposeful ways intrigued her, and so, again in the cafeteria before she had even said hello to Paul Rader, a friend, Chuck Meacham, asked her who she would like to date now that she had had some weeks to look over the crop of available men on campus. Kay looked up and saw Paul standing in line.

"Mmmm, I think I'd like to date Paul Rader," she replied.

The next day Paul asked her to go with him to the Artist Series, and Kay accused Chuck of telling Paul about their cafeteria conversation. Chuck assured her he had not gone near Paul. Any matchmaking was initiated by another source.

At the time Kay didn't realize what an issue The Salvation Army was going to be in this fledgling friendship, but she did know the burn of humiliation when, as she walked into the cafeteria the day after her first date with Paul, a group of friends burst into a raucous chorus of "Put on your old gray bonnet"—a poorly connected reference to bonnets worn by women in The Salvation Army at that time.

Kay couldn't have known at that early juncture that the bonnet was probably the first regularized part of the Army uniform. It appeared in black straw in 1880, according to Edward H. McKinley in *Marching to Glory*, and was designed by co-founder Catherine Booth herself. "Cheap, durable, protective, and solidly unworldly, the bonnet with its red band and huge bow and ribbons became a symbol of the Great Salvation War," McKinley wrote.

But the uninitiated Kay was devastated, unsure of the meaning, even, of her friends' teasing. She knew she would say yes every time Paul suggested they meet for breakfast or take a walk. She knew she fed on the comfort and stimulation of their long discussions about almost everything. But she also knew that The Salvation Army loomed just over Paul's shoulder, and she understood almost nothing about its purpose or its power or what it would mean in her life if she allowed their friendship, their camaraderie, to blossom into love.

It was too much too soon for the 18-year-old girl from rural Georgia, but she didn't want to reject Paul, to send him packing as she had done several less fortunate young men before him. She liked the person very much but wandered within her maze of confusion and questions about the organization to which he was so dedicated.

Back home with her family over Christmas break, Kay spent so much time in tears that her Daddy asked, "Well, what's wrong with this boy?"

"Nothing." she wailed, "and that's the whole problem. But I don't know about The Salvation Army!"

Miss Edith and Mr. Jimmy couldn't help, because they didn't know either. But Mary Jim, graduated from Asbury and married to medical student Jess Lester, her Asbury classmate, could. Mary Jim and Jess knew the Rader three—Jeanne, Damon, Paul—and spoke words that buried themselves in Kay's heart.

"You can't go wrong with this person."

Still she had no clarification about what life within The Salvation Army would mean but could acknowledge that Paul Rader was one of God's chosen and best.

Paul didn't trouble himself about the ramifications of dating a non-Salvationist, and neither did his parents who by this time had been moved back to New York. During the same Christmas when Kay wept through her questions and confusion, after hearing about the girl from Georgia, Lyell Rader recommended to his son that he show her some of the best of The Salvation Army. "Take her to Chicago for the congress." He knew well the excitement and energy that would be generated in one of Chicago's great auditoriums by several thousand Army officers and soldiers. He knew that the music, the banners, and the testimonies could stir the heart of any child of God and that an address by General Wilfrid Kitching would show Kay the thrust, the purpose of the Army in winning God's beloved world to himself.

So they went. Down in front they sat, Paul in his uniform and Kay in a white sequined hat. All during the meeting she stared up at Mrs. General Kitching—in her bonnet.

In spite of all the doubts and questions, neither Paul nor Kay ever dated anyone else. Through subsequent months they both met head on the challenge of their differences. Kay found them frightening; Paul was intrigued. The strength of her personality attracted him, and neither intimidated the other. But resolution and harmony did not come easily. Their conflicts ranged over the cultural differences between North and South, and while each was capable of intensity and focus, they chose different issues upon which to exert these qualities. Harmony was not automatic.

Kay saw goodness and grace in Paul, a firm foundation. She felt enough comfort when she was with him to last a lifetime. She saw a person of true worth, the only person to whom she would ever say, "I love you." She did not tell him so for a time, even after she discovered it was true. She loved Paul but was not sure she could love The Salvation Army.

One night as they said a lingering good-bye on the front steps of Glide-Crawford dormitory, Kay posed a question to Paul: "Would you be willing to do anything else?"

His reply came quickly: "The Army is my life." Kay knew she had to love the Army before she could say she loved Paul.

Even as he declared his ties to The Salvation Army, Paul was daily learning more about the wider Christian community. He didn't say as much, but Kay's question, despite his quick and unequivocal answer, stimulated his investigation of other options. After all, Asbury College was his first exposure to any degree to what other denominations and organizations did in their evangelism efforts, and he wanted to know more. The gospel team trips introduced him to various churches, pastors, and lay believers across America's mid-section. OMS (Oriental Missionary Society) International's Dwight Ferguson, one-time employee and disciple of Paul's great-uncle, Chicago evangelist Paul Rader, liked to visit with the young Paul when he passed through Wilmore and talk to him about worldwide evangelism, about preaching overseas. Ferguson excited Paul's imagination with the broad horizons of international ministry.

When a senior, Paul accepted the job of directing music and youth work at the Methodist church in Paris, Kentucky. Furloughing missionaries often spoke in chapel and stood available for conversation with students. God called Paul into missionary service through OMS's Bill Gilliam, a missionary to Colombia. From these sent out ones he learned about the evangelism, training, church planting, and social work going on under God's leadership around the world.

Even though Paul accepted ministry opportunities in a variety of places and forms, and even though he attended the Wilmore Methodist Church with her occasionally when he was free, Kay didn't know he was open to other ministries. As they dated, she assumed he would be an Army officer, and so would she—if the romance bore the fruit of marriage.

Kay envied the other girls in her dorm. Many of them loved future pastors and missionaries. The demands of this kind of calling seemed so nice and simple and predictable, comfortable in comparison to her relationship with Paul Rader, who, if it progressed, would take her off to training and dress her in ugly shoes and that dreadful bonnet.

All these dreads seemed to come to a head one day when Kay, in her poodle skirt, wide belt and bobby socks, flew through the door of Glide-Crawford dorm, almost crashing into two women in full Army uniform standing in the parlor. In their black stockings, sensible shoes, and bonnets, they took her breath away. She had never encountered women in full Salvation Army uniform that close up. There they were, inches away, in her dorm parlor.

That image stuck with Kay. She pondered training college. What would be required of her? She didn't know, for she had only heard stories, and until now this had not been on the agenda of her long, warm talks with Paul. At such crossroads moments, Kay would initiate cooling-off periods.

"Let's don't eat together for a while," she would suggest, for each day they routinely met and ate all three meals together. "Let's don't date."

Kay needed time and space in which to sort things out, to see how she felt. Each of them always felt saddened by these separations. A few days passed, and they found themselves together again, irresistibly so.

Paul proposed to Kay in her Fort Valley home at the end of the summer before their return to Asbury. In spite of her questions about The Salvation Army and her part in it, Kay knew that Paul was God's gift to her, and she said yes. She also knew that her call to missions, which came during one of Asbury's spontaneous revivals, matched Paul's. The next Christmas vacation she traveled with Paul to the Rader home in New York, where he gave her an engagement ring before they went to an Ice Capades show at Madison Square Garden. Kay didn't see much of the show, captivated as she was by the glitter of the floodlights striking sparks of fire from her diamond.

Paul's parents were taken with Kay. His mother, Gladys, especially liked her, perhaps because she heard the strong-headed, outspoken Kay express herself in ways that she never could. After she learned that Kay enjoyed washing with a new bar of soap, Gladys spoke her regard for the girl from behind her natural reserve by making sure that whenever Kay visited, the guest amenities placed on her bed included a new bar of soap.

The Fullers, on their part, saw their future son-in-law as a treasure. Their kindness and support of him remained throughout the rest of their lives, and Kay's baby brother, Jimbo, adopted Paul as his own, which pleased Kay, because she had discovered early on that Paul loved children. As she listened to his stories about freckle-faced kids at Salvation Army camps, she mused, "This person can go beyond his ego, his macho image, to admit that little kids are important—a not-so-common quality among the men of the early '50s.

On May 29, 1956, Kay Fuller and Paul Rader were married in a ceremony conducted jointly by Rev. J. O. Fuller and Lieutenant Colonel Lyell Rader, the culmination of three years of dating and of praying, conscientiously and intentionally, in search of God's plan for them. They were convinced that whatever the medium for their service, the Lord intended that they discover it together. A scripture used by Colonel Rader in the ceremony could not have been more relevant or significant: "How should one chase a thousand, and two put ten thousand to flight" (Deut. 32:30, KJV).

Under God's guidance and benediction these two linked hearts for the opportunities, the battles, the responsibilities that lay unknown, as yet unidentified, ahead.

1. *Center,* Paul's mother, Gladys, with her parents, Commissioner A. M. Damon and Mrs. Commissioner Annie Damon.
2. The Rader family.
3. The Rader children in 2001: *From left,* Paul, Lyell, Jeanne Gabrielsen, Damon, and Herb.
4. Lt. Col. Lyell M. Rader, O. F., D.D.
5. Mrs. Lt. Col. Gladys Rader.

1. Frances Kay and Mary Jim.
2. *From left,* Frances Kay and Mariah.
3. *From left,* Mary Jim and Kay on a jog by the Thames.

4. The Rev. J. O. Fuller and the Fuller family in the 1940s.
5. The Fuller children. *From left,* Mary Jim, Kay, Edith, and Jim, with Rev. and Mrs. Fuller.

1. Cramped quarters on the *S. S. President Wilson* en route to Korea in 1961.
2. Kay and Paul, with Edic *(center),* J. P., and Jennie in Korean dress.
3. The family in Korea, 1973.

4. Paul and Kay decked out in Korean wedding regalia.

1. Paul and Kay before marriage.
2. Wedding day, May 29, 1956, Estes Chapel at Asbury Theological Seminary, Wilmore, Kentucky.
3. The family in 1981 after Edie *(seated right)* had been away at college for 1½ years.
4. The family at the London Farewell, Westminster Central Hall, July 1999.

4

Real Live Missionaries

THE TRAIN FUSSED ITS WAY into the Seoul station one bitter night in January 1961, its noise and swirling steam amplified by the cold. A family of four—parents in sober Salvation Army uniforms, children bundled against the Korean winter—stepped down from the passenger car and into welcomes by resident officers led by English-born veteran missionaries Colonels Fred and Mable Harvey. Lieutenant Peter Chang stood in the crowd as well, unaware that he and his future wife, Grace, then among the cadets, would become lifelong friends and fellow warriors with the Raders. Training principal Lieutenant Colonel Kwon Kyung-chan mustered all the Korean cadets from the officer training college to swell the welcome party, and they stood on the gritty station platform along with missionary friends from OMS International, some of whom the Raders had known at Asbury College.

Were they cold? Of course. Was this place, this Seoul, Korea, unknown to them? Completely. Did they know what challenges and opportunities awaited them? Not at all. But Paul and Kay Rader, with brand new lieutenant's epaulettes gleaming on their shoulders, were ecstatically happy to be standing in that dingy station so recently cobbled together again after the Korean War. Now true "missionaries," they stood ready to put into action God's call heard back at Asbury College. Due to an exceedingly rough Pacific crossing, getting there was not half the fun, as American advertisers suggest it should be, but it had certainly been achieved under God's guidance and control.

Back in the autumn following their May marriage, the newlywed Raders had returned to Wilmore, Kay to her final two quarters at the college and Paul to Asbury Theological Seminary, situated just across the street, where he, in something of a departure from the norm for potential Salvation Army officers, opted for some theological schooling after his undergraduate work. He knew well that this choice was not part of the usual progression leading up to officer training, but a nudge from the Holy Spirit, "an intimation I might need it," suggested to him it would be a wise move. This choice also forecast a lifelong bent in Paul Rader for study, no more deniable in him than his strong voice or his Salvation Army heritage.

Paul and Kay had not yet applied to go into officer training, had not yet fully decided this was what God wanted for them. Paul still served at the Paris, Kentucky, First Methodist Church with senior pastor Paul Shepherd. He also took his leadership ability and musical skills into evangelism opportunities whenever they arose, even when they intruded on his precious study time.

Shortly after Paul began his theological studies in the fall of 1956, a call for help came from across the street at the college. Dozens of "Sallies" (Salvation Army students) now studied there, including the next Rader, younger brother Herbert, and most of them brought their band instruments with them. But Asbury College, heavily into vocal music and keyboard instruments, had neither instruction nor ensembles for these talented musicians.

"We played together just a short while," Herb Rader remembers, "and we sounded pretty good—but we needed a leader."

This need came into sharp focus because they had been invited to Frankfort, Kentucky, to play publicly, so Herb crossed the street to the seminary to find his big brother amongst his books.

Paul couldn't resist an opportunity to participate yet again in Salvation Army brass band music, so he temporarily closed his precious books and picked up the baton to lead the Asbury College Salvation Army Student Fellowship Band in their first public appearance, a Thanksgiving service at the Frankfort corps.

Attending the celebration was the divisional commander for the southwest Ohio/northeast Kentucky division, William Chamberlain, later national commander. After hearing the polished performance by the band, Chamberlain declared, "They must go to New York!" He meant they should play for the Territorial Music Leaders' Congress.

Back in Wilmore during the intervening months, the student Salvationists and their seminarian bandmaster bore down hard on the finer points of their music, for they would compete against other bands from all over the country.

The hours of practice paid off. After they played and Paul put down his baton and turned to the audience, which contained his former mentor and teacher, Erik Leidzen, it was clear that the Salvation Army Student Fellowship Band from Asbury College had won the respect and appreciation of their audience.

A footnote to their triumph is the fact that decades later, even though Asbury's music division now includes several instrumental ensembles, the distinctive sound of the Salvation Army Student Fellowship Band can still be heard there.

Meanwhile, Captain Andy Miller, the energetic and outgoing divisional youth secretary who must have been pleased with the Raders' work with the band, still felt anxious that they commit their lives to The Salvation Army. He found Paul one day in the seminary library basement studying Hebrew.

"Hey, Paul! What's this?" Miller gestured toward the mysterious print. "For your Jewish converts?"

"Maybe," Paul responded. "I don't really know. I just know I should be here doing this."

Part of Miller's job was to keep tabs on members of the Future Officers Fellowship, which the Raders had joined, and he did so perhaps with more gusto than tact. And while Miller circled and watched and doubtless prayed over this promising young couple, Kay and Paul discussed at length their options. The ease with which they communicated between themselves, discovered during their courtship days, served them well as they pondered aloud their feelings and their search for God's guidance about the matter of their future ministry.

At the same time, Kay strove to be a perfect homemaker—it was the 1950s, after all—and to generate income by her secretarial skills and, after graduation, as a public school teacher by day and Tupperware salesperson by night. Meanwhile, Paul studied.

Taken with the evangelism professor at Asbury Theological Seminary, firebrand, Dr. Robert Coleman, on the way toward his bachelor of divinity degree, Paul wrote a thesis for this mentor titled "The Doctrine of Sanctification in the Life and Work of Charles G. Finney." Finney was a 19th-century evangelist who greatly influenced early Army development.

After graduation from seminary, Paul Rader was not yet through with books and study—and never was, for that matter, throughout his varied ministry career. He heard about Herbert Cross Jackson, well known in mission circles, who was teaching cross-cultural ministries at Louisville's Southern Baptist Seminary. Given his and Kay's call to missionary service and feeling likely this would include leadership training somewhere along the line, Paul thought it best to go to Louisville and acquire a master of theology degree with Jackson as his mentor.

When they moved to Louisville Paul had to sit for entrance exams before his admission to the master's degree program, a requirement that both he and Kay expected would not stand in the way. But on a never-to-be-forgotten day soon after, Kay heard Paul's footsteps on the uncarpeted stairs that led to their walkup apartment. Thud, thud, thud. It could only be Paul, she knew, but what was wrong? He sounded as if he had aged 40 years since breakfast.

Paul walked in and stood staring at his wife.

"Paul—what is it?" Kay asked.

"I failed the exams."

Kay stared at him for a moment; then her eyes snapped with fire. "You couldn't have. You did *not* fail. There's been some mistake, some mix-up. Go right back over there and ask them to double check. This isn't possible."

Kay knew the caliber of academic work to which her husband dedicated himself and therefore she also knew that he was not capable of failure. She closed the door on Paul's retreating back as he headed down the stairs, and then she prayed. Within a short time came footfalls again on the stairs, this time a staccato tap, tap, tap. Paul burst into the room.

"You're right! It *was* a mistake. They mixed up my grades with those of another student. I *did* pass—I'm in!" Two pairs of eyes shone with joy, and two hearts grew stronger in their understanding of God's power exerted on behalf of His obedient servants.

Unruffled by denominational differences between Salvationists and Southern Baptists, Paul did have to grin, however, when a Baptist friend who knew about Army policy regarding the sacraments said, "You ought to pay a heresy fee, coming in here unwashed as you are."

This was a difficult time for Kay as she sought to cope with budget, homemaking, and parenthood. Edie Jeanne, a lively little girl with Rader vocal cords and a mind of her own, rounded out their family, but Kay at times felt depressed over their lack of friends in the new place and their sparse funds to live on, although Paul fortunately acquired generous scholarship support for his graduate study there.

The Shepherds, who pastored the Methodist church in Paris where the Raders worked on staff while at Asbury Theological Seminary, were transferred to Trinity Temple in Louisville. Shepherd offered Paul a job, for he already knew the caliber of ministry of which the young Salvationist was capable. Kay found a teaching job at Finzer Elementary School in the inner city of Louisville, where she learned about child abuse from her pupils, most of whom came from disadvantaged neighborhoods. These encounters reinforced the joy generated in her when she could spread some love among children who received little to none at home.

The Raders spent only a year in Louisville while Paul did the class work required for his master of theology degree and began laboring on his thesis titled "Missionary Strategy in the Post Apostolic Era: 100—313 A.D." Along with lectures, books, and earning a living, they began the lengthy application process for officer training in The Salvation Army, the outcome of the prayer times and discussions characteristic of their relationship. Captain Andy Miller had not been idle during those months. In a letter to Paul's father, then Brigadier Lyell Rader, he told of his woes in trying to get in touch with Paul and Kay because "Major Weyant was concerned about getting material to them so they could get started on their candidate lessons etc."

Miller tried Trinity Temple Methodist Church where Paul worked, and then the Louisville Salvation Army. No address or phone number was available. Finally he kept after the operator until he found Paul's number.

"I talked to him and told him of our concern and our interest in him." Miller brokered the passage of candidate information from Major Weyant to the Raders and then told Brigadier Rader that "I got your lovely letter saying Paul was anxious to get started on his candidate lessons."

Captain Miller obviously cared about Paul, saw in him a young man of worth, and yearned to see him safely within the ranks of his beloved Army. He quoted to Paul's father an excerpt from a letter written by Asbury Theological Seminary Dean W. D. Turkington:

> I wish to say that Mr. Paul Rader was one of the finest young men we have ever had in this institution. He did a most excellent piece of graduate study in the field of theology, received our bachelor of divinity degree, and has gone out for further experience and further graduate study in Southern Baptist Theological Seminary in Louisville, Kentucky. I doubt if it would be possible to find any man who has gone through this institution who has left behind him such a good record in every way as has Paul Rader. His transcript of record will certainly speak for itself as to his character as a student. We recommend him most highly.

For Kay, when she and Paul discussed candidacy in The Salvation Army, their conversations always seemed to come around to her asking Paul, "What do you know best? Where is your heart?" Her knowledge of the Army was by now encyclopedic compared to her first encounter with Paul back at Asbury College. Thanks to the weekends with Captains Morris and Betty Richardson in Frankfort, she knew about open-air forays and how to stand and sing in the rain with drenched hair and the red dye from her songbook cover bleeding down her arm. She had been part of Captain Richardson's offensive against the forces of evil in Frankfort, Kentucky where he fielded more than 400 open-air meetings every year, manned primarily by Asbury College students. This assault netted 147 "decisions at the drumhead" in five year's time. (*Marching to Glory,* 244) Thanks to these weekly experiences, Kay could recognize the smell of vomit mixed with beer. She had smiled and testified her way through the most difficult wards in the local mental hospital and she knew she could do these things, to work with such needy people if God so willed.

After her engagement to Paul, Kay took the public step of joining Richardson's Frankfort corps as a soldier, and so with decision time upon them, her positive exposure to the Army and the people in it made her think, *This probably is best for us.* She knew, too, that it was something in which she would be involved. She had observed wife-of-the-pastor situations as opposed to equal ministry opportunity, member-of-the-team methods in Army officership, and felt drawn to this. She believed The Salvation Army would give her equal opportunity with her husband to work out the realities and ramifications of God's choosing of them both. But even as she affirmed, "I can do this," another part of her wondered, *Can I do this for life? What will be involved? What will I be required to do?*

Then in her constant mulling of the possibilities and questions, Kay thought, *Maybe what I don't like I can get them to change.* Several years passed before Kay learned that *she* was the one who, under God's loving hand, would change, that she couldn't automatically rearrange every circumstance that interfered with her comfort level.

Paul, on the other hand, had gained enough experience outside the familiar warp and woof of The Salvation Army to know that the Army was not the only option open to him, that even though he was born into and shaped by Army mores and ethos, he could function with confidence among the worship and evangelism procedures of the rest of the Evangelical world, preaching, teaching, organizing, leading music, or playing trombone solos even out from under the Army's familiar umbrella—which meant to him that he need never be haunted by the thought that he was a Salvation Army officer because he didn't know how to do anything else.

Having grown up with powerfully committed parents and surrounded by everyone's expectation that he would follow automatically their example, Paul had needed the opportunity to distance himself from their assumptions, to be able to look at life and ministry within The Salvation Army and say without question, "This is what God wants of me." The knowledge that other options stood open to him helped and strengthened him. He knew he was going into the Army because this was what God wanted, not because he had to.

So the Raders sat down with the lessons sent them, the exercises that initiated the application process. They filled out the same forms and took the same tests for application. The requirements were identical for each of them.

Accepted as cadets, with daughter Edie in tow, the Raders reported to the School for Officer Training in the Bronx, New York, to begin their preparation for officership as members of the Soldiers of Christ Session. This year, 1960, was the first that the length of officer training was expanded to two years from its previous nine months. (Edward McKinley describes this change in *Marching to Glory*, 265). They plunged into the classes and field work, which included marches and open-air meetings, multiple forms of evangelism, and selling *The War Cry,* the venerable Army magazine.

Everything came to an abrupt halt, however, when toward the end of their first year in training Paul received a summons from the Field Secretary, Lieutenant Colonel Albert Pepper, to appear at headquarters on Manhattan's 14th Street. In late November of 1960, the Raders had written a letter to their training principal, Lieutenant Colonel Emil Nelson, which said in part,

> Some four years ago the Lord laid upon our hearts a compelling concern for foreign missions. Although we had been deeply interested in missions for some time, it was then that the Lord made His purpose for us unmistakably plain. A whole complex of factors was involved in our calling: circumstances, significant contact with missionaries, growing awareness of needs, experiences in prayer, the direction and illumination of the Spirit in the study of the Word. My wife

and I were gripped with this divine compulsion simultaneously, though on an individual basis.

The conviction that God has called us to foreign missionary service has only deepened in the last four years. The commitment to some part in the task of world evangelization has been the supreme motivation and the focal center of all our efforts in preparation.

Army leadership responsible for the 1960 session of cadets paid attention to the letter and to the fact that the Raders were older and more highly trained than most in their session and therefore possible candidates to fill one of a couple of openings for officers in Japan or Korea. Colonel Pepper described the appointment opportunities to Cadet Rader: one for youth work in Japan and one for officer training in Korea. "How do you feel about them?" he inquired.

"We'll go to Korea," Paul answered.

"Better go home and pray about it."

"I'll be happy to go home and talk with Kay about it, and, of course, we'll pray, but I'm pretty sure that's what it's going to be."

Pray and talk they did, and then the next day Paul phoned Colonel Pepper and told him that Korea was their choice.

Part of what made the choice so easy was Paul's friendship at Asbury Theological Seminary with another Paul—Paul Chung Ching-kyung—a Korean fellow student at Asbury Seminary who said one day as they both studied in the seminary library, "You must come to my country one day."

"If God calls us," was Rader's reply. And eventually, as a guest professor, Paul Rader taught in OMS-founded Seoul Theological Seminary where Paul Chung served as professor and administrator.

Another factor which made Korea a standout appointment possibility for Paul Rader was that during his college gospel team days he had dozens of times watched the film *38th Parallel,* produced by World Vision founder Bob Pierce, which the team used as part of their weekend presentations. Each time he saw the scenes of wartime devastation that painted a backdrop for Korean

Christians' strong courage and faith, it moved him deeply. (Years later Bob Pierce, on a visit to Korea, told Paul, "All the theology I ever learned I got from Paul Rader," for Pierce was yet another one from the crop of Christian leaders imprinted for God by Paul's great uncle in Chicago.)

Paul's conversation with Field Secretary Pepper took both Rader cadets by surprise, and they pondered it in wonderment in spite of the quickness and surety of Paul's reply. Yet another deciding factor in their choice was the business of language study. With astuteness beyond their cross-cultural experience at that point, they considered language learning. They figured that youth work in Japan, as in any country, would require understanding a constantly changing teenage lingo, a subculture within a culture they had yet to learn, which, they surmised, would be a heavy load for novice missionaries to handle. Korea, on the other hand, meant working with cadets in officer training who, they assumed, had to listen whether or not their teachers did well in the language. This leverage for newcomers would offer some leeway in the pace and skill with which they learned to communicate. And pragmatism aside, both Raders had done youth work in the United States and found themselves leaning toward the more predictable structure of the classroom coupled with the joyful challenge of participating in the preparation of future officers.

They decided for the cadets—and chose the Korea appointment.

With the decision made and training abruptly terminated, Kay and Paul moved in with the senior Raders for a few months while they packed and prepared to travel to Korea, while Paul went to the Berlitz language institute to gain some grasp of Korean speech and thought, and while a second child, James Paul Rader, added himself to their family.

Paul and Kay, appointed as cadet lieutenants at the conclusion of the first year of training, were told, "When you get on the ship in California, you'll change your rank insignia and disembark as second lieutenants." A letter from Commissioner Holland French, eastern territorial commander, confirmed this. He wrote,

> Word has come to hand from the International Secretary

stating that, in view of your leaving for Missionary Service, the General has agreed to your status now being that of fully commissioned officers with the rank of Lieutenant. This promotion to be effective as of December 4, 1961.

We feel sure that you will receive this rank as an evidence of confidence on the part of your leaders and will be a source of encouragement to you.

May God abundantly bless you and grant you every need for the tasks that are before you.

Prior to any leaving, however, was the business of purchasing and packing whatever a family of four would need in Korea. Fumbling along with minimal information, they managed this feat in conjunction with the baby's arrival, Paul's language work, their temporary appointment to the Newark, New Jersey corps, all of which ended when they boarded a plane for California. But before leaving New York, Paul received a poignant and articulate letter of farewell from elder brother Damon, who was already appointed to the Usher Institute in then Southern Rhodesia. He wrote,

We rejoice with you in your appointment to the training staff in Korea. We thank God for your clear-cut commitment to Him . . . the sweet fragrance of His knowledge will be graciously evident wherever you go.

The disciplines and "dog-work" and denials that inescapably lie ahead will, I know, only drive you to greater dependence and devotion to the Faithful One who goes with you. . . . You may find, as I have, how much harder it is to be "nothing" for God than something.

Damon went on to advise his brother against preconceived ideas, about interpersonal problems and other irritants inherent to missionary service. Then he expressed his affection.

I am sure you know how I love you, and how proud I am to belong to the same family. . . . We are a bit sad at the prospect of not seeing you folks again for a long time, if ever, but this is more than offset by the knowledge of your joy in doing the Divine Will. . . . God bless you superabundantly, dear brother, and give you all necessary Grace.

Grace was needed aplenty as Paul, Kay, Edie, and J. P. transferred from airport to the *President Wilson,* a passenger ship of the American President Lines, where they stuffed their four selves into a tiny cabin below the water line, which shared a bulkhead with the rumbling engine room. Given the lack of any shelf or dresser top, a farewell bouquet had to perch in the miniature washbasin behind the door. Baby J. P. slept in a dresser drawer.

Waves and wind mistreated the ship all across the Pacific, and some of her passengers suffered as well. She eventually disgorged her tired, her sick, and her claustrophobic in Yokohama, Japan, on Christmas Eve, and the Rader family spent the holiday in a Salvation Army hostel for Japanese girls. In true missionary fashion, however, they came prepared with gifts for each other and reminders for them all of the Savior's birth, thereby creating a circle of warmth and love and worship in the strangest place they had ever been—until then.

Only the crossing of the straits between Japan and Korea remained then between them and the port of Pusan on the southern tip of the Korean peninsula, where, guided by Brigadier George Engle, an American officer who had come down from Seoul to help, they saw their baggage through customs and loaded onto the train that took them to Seoul—not a task for the fainthearted—and the adventures that God readied for them there.

5

On the Go, On the Grow

THE CITY OF SEOUL, into which the Raders stepped that cold January night in 1961, was capital to one half of a sundered nation suffering, as all war-torn countries suffer, from the brutal, destructive conflict that had raged for three years up and down the peninsula. After the Yalta Conference, in which Winston Churchill, Franklin Roosevelt, and Joseph Stalin, victors of World War II, divided up huge portions of the globe, Korea, until then a Japanese colony, stood divided along the 38th parallel with the northern half under Russian control, while the United Nations (with the United States providing the major portion of men and materiel) took over the south.

Within five years, in June 1950, war broke out between north and south when Communist-indoctrinated North Korean troops backed by the Chinese attacked fellow countrymen in the south in an attempt to reunite the nation under one ideology—theirs. The story of the next three years of holocaust and destruction can be read in other books, but the results still lay heavy upon the land in 1961. Yes, the rubble had been removed, the dead mourned and buried, but refugees, many still homeless, fought for survival from their scrap heap hovels. Beggars roamed the streets, many of them disabled and disfigured war veterans. Homeless individuals froze to death each and every night during Korea's frigid winters.

The South Korean economy lay in shambles. Leathery-faced women who looked like heaps of rags and waste paper as they huddled under layers of whatever protection they could scavenge sat by the streets offering for sale roasted sweet potatoes to hurrying passersby; a small child, even, could be shivering beneath the detritus that sheltered its mother. Almost the only traffic in those days on Seoul's boulevards consisted of oxen, ponies—or men—pulling cartloads of coal briquettes, straw bags of rice, or cabbages from the country. Little black Jeeps belonging to government officials competed for road space with snorting, lopsided public buses whose bodies had been hammered out of military surplus steel drums and set on the chassis of captured Russian-made Army trucks.

Little food showed up in the markets aside from cabbage, potatoes, rice, carrots, and apples. Consumer goods from other nations did not appear on shop shelves during those times. Mountains and hillsides throughout the peninsula were scraped bare of every stick, tree, or blade of dry grass and consumed for fuel. Survival was top priority for the impoverished majority of 30 million desperate people.

God was there, however, sheltering, strengthening, and enabling His children, making it possible for two young Salvation Army officers to feel "ecstatically happy" to be in Korea in spite of her problems and frequent pathos. After all, they were fulfilling the Lord's imperative to each of them that they take His good news to His beloved world, which is what they intended to do in Korea, their appointed place in that world.

Arriving with appointments to the Officer Training College, their first priority was to master the language. Thanks to his weeks at Berlitz in New York (an Army experiment), Paul enjoyed an advantage in that he had a small vocabulary and some inkling of the grammar pitfalls that awaited them both. His brief, carefully constructed greeting at their welcome service—in Korean—surprised and delighted those who heard it.

Paul soon went off to the Korean Language Institute at Yonsei University, one of Korea's most prestigious centers of learning, where he spent four hours each day in class. Then he dedicated his afternoons to working with a tutor perfecting what he had covered in the morning classes. Commissioner Peter Chang remembers those years of language learning, for he, an unmarried lieutenant then, lived just next door at the training college: "With Paul, when he studied something, it would consume his total concentration. He would hardly even notice anything else around him."

Kay was required to follow a different path toward learning Korean. Their leaders decided that because the Raders had two small children who were new to the country, Kay should stay home with them, a pattern followed by many mission boards at that time. A tutor came to help. Lee YongWha spent four to five hours per week teaching her to read and write and speak. She reported to Territorial Commander Commissioner Frederick Harvey her test grades and the amount of progress she made.

It didn't take long, however, for Kay to sense the inadequacy of this plan, her few hours per week up against Paul's eight hours or so each day. She was being left far behind in this crucial enterprise. A conversation with the Commissioner about the discrepancy revealed a basic difficulty: the budget couldn't stretch around a stepped-up study program for Kay. Disappointed, she didn't yield to defeat but got out paper and stamps and raised "non-Army" money for more tutor hours from people at home. She acquired another advantage in that both Edie and J. P. adjusted rapidly and happily to life among the people around them and didn't need their mother's constant presence. Helpers, staff, and their children became playmates and caregivers to the two small Raders, teaching the little newcomers both culture and language in arguably the best school of all.

Kay therefore got her turn at the Yonsei University language institute and soon caught up with her husband in fluency and comprehension. And then came the next challenge, teaching assignments in the officer training program located in the building next door to their home. It was time to test their fledgling language skills in the crucible of the classroom.

The Salvation Army built an impressive structure in 1925 modeled after Clapton Congress Hall, the training college in London. Bramwell Booth, famed son of founder William Booth, turned 70 in 1925 and the building celebrates his birthday. Its pillars and well-proportioned windows face out onto a street lined with monuments and memories. Just across the way is the American ambassador's residence. Until a newer home was built, the classic nobleman's villa in use so long was touted to be one of the oldest residences in United States diplomatic service. Over the wall from the ambassador's residence on one side, buzzing like a hive of angry bees, lies the long-established and prestigious Pae-che Girls' High School. Up the other way stands an old red brick church, the Chung Dong Methodist Church, first Protestant worship center ever built in Korea and a beloved monument to God's grace for countless Korean Christians. Add to this the tile-roofed palace compound where Korea's last reigning king presided over the ceaseless scrap between Japan and China as to who would control his kingdom, where his queen was murdered and from which he fled when war finally erupted. From their beginnings at the onset of the 20th century, The Salvation Army, as usual, managed to plant the flag in the thick of whatever battle raged over the interests and loyalties of men and women in that place.

Paul took on classes in Old Testament and evangelism in rooms that looked out on this centuries-old heart of Seoul; Kay taught English (hunger for this international *lingua franca* inflamed all young Koreans) and Christian education. They team taught music. But the assignment that perhaps stretched them the most by learning as they led was their supervision of cadets' field work, which added to their language skills and taught them at warp speed the ins and outs of Korean culture.

The cadets were divided into brigades and went out into the field mid-week, weekends, and for spring "boom marches," a term coined by Salvationists in India that caught on throughout the Army. Field forays occurred usually under the auspices of a Salvation Army corps, or church, where the future officers watched and learned and asked questions of the corps officers already on site before they tried their hands at ministry on their own.

Each Rader took responsibility for a brigade. Kay's contingent developed ongoing ministry with a corps in Shillim Dong, a bleak refugee area south of the Han River. Here the corps officers, Lieutenants Pak CheTek and Chung ChungSuk and their little family, lived in a curtained-off section of the United States

Army surplus tent, which was the worship sanctuary for the poverty-blighted people who came there to find God. Inside the tent a sawdust-burning stove warmed a small space, and since it generated the only heat in the neighborhood, people came to the corps to get warm, physically at first, and then, some of them, spiritually. The tent stood at the top of a steep hill, and since the bus stopped far down below, Kay and her brigade scrambled up to it through seasons of snow and ice, monsoon downpours, and oppressive heat. Finding herself winded and unfit for the climb, activist Kay embarked on a Canadian 5BX exercise program, popular at the time, determined to fulfill her responsibilities unhampered by aching muscles and shortness of breath.

In true Salvation Army style, Lieutenants Pak and Chung (married women keep their own family names in Korea) and the cadet brigade surveyed the neighborhood around their tent temple to discover how best to minister to the people there. Day care for babies and children, they discovered, was crucial for parents who earned a meager living by selling items on the street, by digging through dumps for salable scrap, by hiring out their bent backs and sinewy arms to haul goods between markets and the homes of those who could afford such service.

And those babies in day care in Shillim Dong needed milk. Again, some well-planned telling of the Shillim Dong story stimulated enough donations to buy a couple of goats, which the Raders loaded into a vehicle, hauled to the foot of the hill, and then persuaded and pushed up the slope so the babies could have their life-sustaining milk.

The corps at Shillim Dong thrived, so much so that Lieutenant Pak and his little band of Salvationists began to dream about constructing a real church building, knowing that all they lacked were the funds to make it possible. Meanwhile, Paul, while perusing a stray copy of *Reader's Digest,* came upon an article about a simple brick-making machine that he persuaded the America Korea Foundation to supply. Side by side with the people of the hilltop corps, cadets and staff tore into brick making, and finally a sturdy little structure replaced the tattered old tent.

During one visit as Kay and her brigade gazed with pride at

the new building, she asked Lieutenant Pak a question. "What do you need now, Lieutenant?"

"We need water," came his prompt reply. "The people up here have none. We've searched the hillside and can't find any."

Kay turned away from Pak as she pondered the problem. Her gaze lit upon a trickle of water near a corner of the new building. She pointed.

"What's that?"

Lieutenant Pak stared open-mouthed. "I never saw *that* before! We've looked everywhere." By then Kay knew what to do.

"I'll go home and write some letters or do something to raise the money for the well," she promised, "if you'll get your young people to do the digging."

Done. The Raders raised the money, the corps young people dug the well, and the community learned another lesson about God's power and grace, about His potent, practical love for them.

General Wilfred Kitching, far away in London at the Army's international headquarters, paid attention to the newsletters sent out by the Raders that told some of the stories like this in an effort to stimulate prayer support for their ministries. In 1963 Paul had written about the great hole that would be left in Korea if there were no Salvation Army. General Kitching wrote in response, "My dear Lieutenant, I want to tell you that your circular letter dated 'Summer' was a very moving epistle to me. The General [apparently a modest personal reference] could well add if the Raders were not in Seoul what a hole the Army would be in. I thank you very sincerely for all that you are doing, and I send you my warm personal greetings."

In 1966 General Kitching wrote again: "I have just been reading your December letter and of course with much interest. It is always a pleasure to read of your activities, and though I have not been in the habit of writing, I have ever since you arrived in Korea followed your activities with much interest and prayer."

Both Raders came to Korea with a high level of cultural sensitivity, which enabled them to avoid many of the gaffes and missteps committed by missionaries throughout the centuries. As Commissioner Chang remembers, "The coming of Paul and Kay to Korea was simply like a breath of fresh air. . . . Their genuine and sincere approach to Koreans made a very lasting impression upon many Salvationists in Korea."

How did they acquire such rare and remarkable skills?

Paul's came partially via academics. His classes in missions at Southern Baptist Theological Seminary were presented with respect and objectivity. Add to this his growing up amid the rich racial and religious mix in the New York area, which helped to make him comfortable in Korea. People different from him were nothing new.

Kay's growing-up experiences in Georgia forged a love for Mariah, her African-American caregiver and friend, along with others like her at Mr. Jimmy's mission. And then during officer training in New York, her favorite field training supervisor was an African-American officer, Major (later Lieutenant Colonel) B. Barton MacIntyre, who was in charge of the Army's work in Harlem. His order to his charges was clear: "Don't *ever* say 'you people' when you get up to speak or testify here, or even in conversation!" Thanks in part to him and to her upbringing, Kay knew how to talk with Blacks, with Asians, with anyone different from herself; to enjoy food that never appeared on the Fuller table; and to be comfortable and unthreatened in unfamiliar situations.

Peter Chang describes their demeanor among the people as being "very sensitive to the feelings of the Koreans. . . . Paul and Kay would learn all the right things to do . . . and did them, all the time . . . while they made themselves one with us as Koreans, eating and enjoying Korean meals, attempting to do everything the way it was done in Korea, so they earned great respect and much love from their fellow officers and comrades. We know they did it because they really loved the Lord and The Salvation Army. This was their calling."

Chang's astute observation skills missed little for he decided that perhaps "Paul was sometimes too sensitive so as not, if at all possible, to be offending. How difficult it must have been! Paul has a good sense of humor, plenty of it, yet he was always very careful not to be misunderstood. In fact, to a point, Paul was probably overcareful."

Added to the mix were two unique individuals who served as mentors to the Raders, molding their attitudes, demeanor, and spiritual development especially during their first decade as missionaries and Salvation Army officers.

Lieutenant Colonel Kwon Kyung-chan served his Army and his Savior as training principal for over 20 years and therefore was responsible for the Raders by virtue of their appointment to the training college. Kwon loomed large during their tenure there as he supervised their service with the cadets. Son of a village leader who was a person of substance, Kwon had the advantage of a classical Confucian/Korean education, making him the ideal example of how polished and proper Koreans do things. A man of elegance and fine Asian manners, he often spoke to his officer trainees on the best way to do things, and the Raders listened carefully, for they respected him and sensed that what he had to say would profit them and their ministry in Korea.

Kwon took his responsibility for the young missionaries seriously, showing up at their door for every child's birthday and every holiday saying, as his wife handed over a small token gift, "We know you have no grandparents here, so we came to wish you well."

The Colonel subtly nudged Paul ever onward in his language acquisition, using the Thursday open-air service as his venue for encouraging Paul's public use of the tangled web of Korean speech. Paul might be standing quietly aside as the Koreans shared and sang for passersby on Seoul's busy streets, aside, that is, until Kwon turned to him and said for all to hear, "Lieutenant Rader has come from the United States. Tell me, Lieutenant—why did you come to Korea? What is your work here?"

Those were questions that language students grapple with and learn answers to early on in their studies but are terrifying to be forced to respond to before a sidewalk full of dark-eyed strangers staring at your height, your strangely colored eyes, and your high-bridged nose.

By consistent example Colonel Kwon taught Paul some of the precepts of what it meant to be in charge in The Salvation Army. His record of courage and faithfulness in guarding Army property in Seoul during the occupation by the North Korean forces spoke loudly as did the gentle charisma he exuded as he led his young American officers through the labyrinth of access routes to the heart of Korean Salvationism. The Raders saw in the Colonel a man of kindness, exuberance, and mature decisions, always the boss but graciously, elegantly in charge. Few of the cadets he trained ever left the Army.

The Raders connected with another mentor, an American this time, at Seoul Union Church, a venerable institution as old in Korea as the Protestant missionary endeavor itself. At that time, the congregation gathered at 4 P.M. each Sunday afternoon in a Methodist center near downtown Seoul to study and be ministered to by each other. Paul and Kay discovered a Bible class during the Sunday School hour led by Presbyterian veteran Harold Voelkel and found it to be stimulating indeed, just what they needed to recharge their spiritual batteries after a week packed with ministry of their own.

Voelkel, after 40 years of missionary service, was a local legend because of what he did beyond the predictable teaching and preaching and sitting in on decision-making committees. During and shortly after the Korean War, Voelkel gained entry to the camps where North Korean prisoners of war huddled, awaiting their fate. There, in a style that could provoke envy in a fiery Salvationist's heart, he preached to thousands of defeated, displaced men, exuberantly pointing them to the Savior, who alone could turn their defeat into eternal victory.

But he didn't stop with evangelizing. Voelkel exhorted his prisoner congregations to serve their newfound Redeemer, and when hundreds agreed, he set up Bible studies, even seminaries, to disciple and train them for ministry.

Always on the lookout for leadership material, when Voelkel spotted Paul and Kay Rader at Union Church, the next thing they knew they were headed across town to dine with the Voelkels on the Presbyterian compound. Usually the youngest people at the table for many such meals, the Raders did lots of listening as other missionary veterans of the Voelkels' vintage talked of Korea and their work. Their frequent dinners led to Paul's invitation to a Monday morning men's prayer meeting—at 6 A.M. Harold Voelkel knew that here was a young man with God's imprint upon him, and he wanted to do his part in ensuring that Paul's steps were unerringly aimed in the right direction.

Language acquisition was one of Voelkel's pet issues. So at one of Harold and Gertrude's get-togethers when he asked Paul what he had been doing lately, Paul began to tell with relish about preaching an evangelistic campaign at one of the city corps. Voelkel fixed Paul with a wary stare.

"How did you do that?" he queried, knowing that Paul was still struggling at Yonsei with Korean verb endings.

"Well, Peter Chang translated—"

Voelkel backed his apprehensive disciple up against the living room wall.

"Don't *ever* do that again!" he roared, shaking his finger in Paul's face.

The best Paul could squeeze out at the moment was a limp "Really?"

"If you start doing that you'll *never* learn to preach in Korean. You must never preach again until you learn to do it in Korean."

Harold Voelkel had seen too many missionaries succumb to the expedient under the pressure of having so much to do, using interpreters and getting by rather than buckling down to learn to speak in Korean on their own.

Voelkel's disciple took his mentor seriously—how could he not?—and never again lifted his Bible and his voice before a Korean audience until he could do it in the language of their hearts. Fortunately, that didn't take too long.

Meanwhile the Raders poured themselves into their teaching and supervisory roles and trekked across the city and into the countryside with their cadets several days each month for field training. Because on those days they both stayed out all day long, that meant their children—Edie, J. P., and by now Jennie, born just before Christmas in 1964—required special thought. Kay donned her mother's cap and made sure the days of their absence held plenty of joy and comfort for their children. She baked cookies and plotted treasure hunts complete with handwritten clues, seeking to avoid any dread that could arise in their hearts when they came home from school and found both parents gone. God blessed the Rader family with good home helpers in those days, people they could trust with their dearest treasures. All three children knew they were thought of and planned for. And because Paul and Kay maintained contacts and friendships among the people of the missionary community in Seoul, the Rader children did not lack for Western playmates along with the Korean children just outside their door.

The tempo of their days picked up speed as each of them added to their list of responsibilities. The issue of transportation around the sprawling capital and out into the countryside for Kay and Paul vacillated between irritating and crucial. Some missions had small fleets of boxy, battered vehicles bought for durability rather than comfort, and these banged over Korea's rutted roads as the missionaries traveled out to teach, to evangelize, and to meet with committees. The Salvation Army, however, had no such fleet, only one or two cars for the use of senior officers.

Paul and Kay caught taxis to go to language school or church, for marketing or for meetings. They rode public buses when on field forays with their brigades, all of which got the job done to a degree, but they still had to grapple with the time-consuming inadequacies of no readily available transportation.

So Paul bought a Honda motorcycle, learned the basics of managing it, and became a familiar sight around the city. After all, not too many towering foreigners in dark blue uniforms wearing white helmets roared through Seoul's thickening traffic on motorcycles, especially with a bright red box bolted on behind the seat.

One winter day a knock sounded through the Raders' quarters, and Kay opened the door to be confronted by a woman she didn't know.

"Do big-nosed foreigners live here?"

"Yes, we do."

"Does a big-nosed man who rides a motorcycle live here?"

By now Kay's well-honed intuition told her that something

was terribly wrong, so she thrust her feet into her shoes that lay closest to the door—a pair of three-inch heels—and started to run up the street in the direction from which Paul would be riding on his way home from the post office on the United States Army base.

She came upon the spot in the street where broken glass and blood lay in the shadow of an ancient palace wall. But she saw no Paul, no motorcycle. On she churned down another street that branched off toward a small private hospital where someone might have taken a foreign accident victim. Kay burst through the clinic door and began querying white-coated personnel.

"Did anyone bring a big foreign man here? An accident victim?"

No, they had not seen such an individual. A thankful Kay felt a flicker of hope. Did this mean that Paul had been able to request he be taken to Severance Hospital, a joint mission project where he would be sure to receive good care? *Please, God, let it be so.*

Kay found Paul still in the emergency room at Severance, the victim of a head-on collision with a large truck that had roared through a gate and up the narrow street, going the wrong way. Along with multiple cuts and bruises, he had one badly injured leg and a foot gouged from when the Honda spun out of control as he struggled to avoid the collision.

Paul made it to Severance, because in spite of being struck head-on, he never lost consciousness. The guilt-ridden truck driver flagged a cruising taxi and told the man behind its wheel to take the battered, bleeding American for help.

"No, no—not in my car. He'll get blood all over everything!"

Probably accustomed to menacing his way through from behind the wheel to what he wanted, the truck driver persuaded the taxi driver that he would be wise to do as he asked. The two of them bundled the six-foot, three-inch foreigner—blood and all—into the taxi's back seat.

"Take me to Severance Hospital," Paul muttered.

There Kay, following her God-given instincts, found her husband.

Paul's accident and 13-day hospital stay threw a wrench into some very important works then under development between The Salvation Army and the United States Army. Because the Commissioners Harvey and Colonels Engel were on furlough, the responsibility for a Christmas kettle campaign on the military headquarters base was left to the Raders. Negotiations with the chaplain's office to expand the Christmas effort more widely than ever were coming together satisfactorily. The GIs would hear the bells and see the famous red kettles outside their PXs, commissaries, theaters, and libraries and have the chance to turn their nostalgia into tangible help for the work of The Salvation Army in Korea.

But Paul lay in the hospital immobilized by a badly wounded leg, and the motorcycle that took him from place to place was no more. What would become of the campaign?

Kay saw that she had to take over or see the Christmas campaign die. Which meant orphans, babies, widows, corps—all The Salvation Army projects—would suffer in some way if those bells didn't ring.

So rolling up her sleeves and moving just a little faster, without a car to get her around the city, Kay saw to it that ringers staffed every kettle on the base and included herself on that roster. She counted money with the chaplain's staff with nearly frostbitten fingers, which ever after remained painfully sensitive to cold, answered questions, and dealt on her own with each issue that arose.

Kay took her turn standing kettles, and then when all was finished, she piloted the band from the Korean Boys Home on a carolling tour to bars and clubs on the sprawling post as well as embassies across the city. In the wee hours of the morning she returned home to complete her own family's Christmas preparation.

A sequel to those difficult times brought blessing to the Rader family and an easement to their transportation woes. Letters home to the States stimulated family, Mary Jim and husband Jess, to donate toward a car, and before many months passed, they had their own royal blue Toyota Land Cruiser chariot to get them where they needed to be.

Missionary fellowship and networking flowed around several focal points, and the Raders, true to their patterns back in the United States, drew benefits from the wider community that aided in their Salvation Army ministry and strengthened their own personal lives as well. At Seoul Union Church (which soon discovered Paul's extraordinary preaching gifts and Kay's teaching ability and utilized them regularly), the Rader family enjoyed the oasis time of worship in their own language, of praying and sharing with fellow missionaries who pursued the same goals and struggled with the same problems as did they.

Added to the church was Seoul Foreign School, also founded by the earliest Protestant pioneers in the late 19th century, of which the very first graduate was Minnie French Wiseman, a Salvationist daughter of early territorial leaders. Here the Rader children, one by one, began their formal education in English with plenty of Korean culture thrown in. Their Korean language skills flourished outside their front door because of their playmates, the cadets, and the staff people with whom they came in daily contact.

During Korea's long, hot, humid summers, many in the expatriate community spent some days at Taechon Beach, a spit of piney land with shell-laden beaches on the west coast south of Seoul. Here the missionaries built a remarkable collection of cabins reminiscent of those on some of America's camp meeting grounds. Here they rested and wrote reports and swam and exchanged ideas by sunlight, moonlight, and kerosene lamplight, on the beach or beside the tennis court. Time to heal, time to think—and time to serve on the committees that kept the place functioning.

Kay and Paul enjoyed warm, rich times with extended family as well, because in the fall of 1962 Paul's sister Jeanne Gabrielsen, with her surgeon husband Ted and their three children—Campbell, Jill, and Beth Marie—came to Korea under appointment to The Salvation Army hospital in Yong Dong. This small town lay south of Taejon, a city several hours south of Seoul.

Because of distance, dubious transportation, and heavy schedules, visits were irregular and widely spaced, but when they happened, with six children and four adults snug together in quarters designed for fewer people (to say the least), love, laughter, and shoptalk outweighed the logistical problems—most of the time.

Both Raders remember, "It was wonderful to have family to be part of the venture." Paul and Ted pooled their skills and love for Korea in what they called the "Bible and Black Bag" campaign, taking evangelism and medicine to the country folk who lived in the vicinity of Yong Dong.

The Gabrielsens' ministry through the Army hospital soon made them well known and respected persons in Yong Dong and surrounding areas. For a time Jeanne filled in for the hospital's depleted nursing staff even to the point of kneeling and washing a leper's feet. At first Ted's makeshift operating table stood on stacks of bricks for height as he peered through the shadows under the single light bulb dangling from the ceiling. When General Frederick Coutts came from London to inspect Army troops and installations in Korea, all of Yong Dong turned out to welcome him, waving tiny homemade Salvation Army flags and lining the roadways as if for a royal procession. If he was responsible for the missionary family in their town, they wanted him to know they were glad he came.

New ideas and issues stirred in Paul Rader's mind and heart toward the end of the '60s. At Taechon Beach, on his rounds in Seoul, and over dinners with other missionaries, Paul began to compare what he was learning about the growth of churches in other denominations with the growth of Salvation Army corps, and he didn't like what he saw. After all, as intensely involved as he and Kay were with officer training and grappling with the problem of too many cadets for too few appointments, they needed to know why the Salvation Army wasn't growing and what could be done about it. Paul mulled the issue over with the single-minded intensity for which he was becoming well known. They had to find some answers.

6

Put Up the Shutters or Catch the Wave?

THIS MIGHT BE THE ANSWER. Just the ticket for the statistical stagnation in which Korea's Salvation Army lay mired as the decade of the '60s drew to its end.

So thought Paul Rader as he closed Donald McGavran's *How Churches Grow* on his finger and stared unseeing across the room. Church growth theories popped up before him everywhere he turned, it seemed, especially in his reading—in the journals that made their laborious way to Seoul via sea mail, in almost every book he could borrow from his Methodist, OMS, Baptist, and Presbyterian colleagues or received as gifts from friends and family back home. And here, in McGavran's book, reading about the apostle Paul's apostolic mission fired his heart, as did the guidelines for persuading people to become Christian disciples. This read like something William Booth might have written. The way McGavran dealt with the tension between social services and grassroots evangelism spoke to the issues that he had mulled over and over again. This was it!

Fuller Theological Seminary's fledgling Institute of Church Growth was generating a remarkable amount of dialog within the Evangelical world, and the more he learned about the fresh thinking and breakout theories emanating from those associated with the Institute, the more Captain Paul (promoted in 1966) thought they might provide some answers for The Salvation Army in Korea.

After all, Korean churches were growing at a prodigious rate, but the number of Salvation Army corps had not changed since immediately following the Korean War. The number of corps had grown from 57 in 1950 to 101 in 1960. The number of soldiers had advanced from 3,580 to 10,300 over the same period. The Army almost quadrupled their community in 10 years—and then stopped dead while other denominations moved ahead planting new congregations, shepherding new believers (Paul Rader, "The Salvation Army in Korea after 1945: A Study in Growth and Self Understanding," doctoral dissertation, Fuller Theological Seminary, 1973). This didn't make sense to Paul, because, corps or church, the adherents were all Korean with the same economics brought into play, the same problems plaguing them, and the same opportunities beckoning. And most important, the same God listened to their prayers and poured out his love over all.

At that time Salvation Army leadership believed the only way to grow was to acquire money from International Headquarters in London. Korea still struggled economically because of the war (although matters improved step by laborious step), and one couldn't expect the believers in each corps to do too much in the way of self-support, now could one? And even if they did come up with some token funds on their own, this would care only for the existing corps and would certainly never provide anything for growth. Certainly not.

But the fact remained that far more Korean young people felt called to be officers and were applying for training than could be accepted, and here is where the problem intersected in a most practical manner with Kay and Paul, who were appointed to and involved in the training of cadets. Why not accept more applicants? For the simple reason that once accepted, the Army assumed responsibility for their allowances and certain small entitlements, but without new corps being planted—and the frustrating question seems best articulated in New York patois: What're ya gonna do with all these people?

It's an Army fact of life that trained officers are entitled to an appointment, but in Korea appointments didn't exist, and the financial secretary saw no funds either on their books or slated to arrive from London to sustain all the cadets who wanted to train for the Army's war against sin.

Paul listened to the candidate council's report, to the disparity between applicants and those accepted, and in his mind he stared at the ranks of potential officers wondering what should be done with them much as he had plotted over his tiny soldiers on his mother's kitchen table.

"Well, let's take care of our levels of attrition, watch the actuarials down the line, maintain the status quo, and we'll train replacements—that's all." So the argument went from those faced with a static budget and no hope of an increase, for appeals to International Headquarters produced no help. The status quo worked out to somewhere between 10 and 20 cadets per session, and 10 to 20 cadets meant five to 10 units or ministry teams, since in Korea marriage was required of cadets with very few exceptions. Accept just enough to maintain the status quo, but no one to expand frontiers or foster growth.

Counterarguments roiled in Paul's thinking, for he knew that their training staff put their all into the small sessions each year when the same amount of effort could equip twice as many officers for the salvation war. The Raders were so bold as to talk with the Harveys about what was happening, but no channel existed for junior officers such as they to make appeals themselves. Talk proved futile, and their hearts sank further as they heard Commissioner Rusher predict that, according to his reading of the statistics, soon perhaps there would no longer be a Salvation Army in Korea. This frustrated Paul, and he chewed on the problem like a terrier with an oversized bone.

Meanwhile, the Raders' OMS friends spoke of booming growth within the Korea Holiness Church, the indigenous denomination begun some 50 years earlier by that faith mission within one year of the Army's "opening fire" in the peninsula. Methodists and Presbyterians, in spite of political scraps and schisms, also saw new churches blooming like dandelions across the country with only token assistance from their parent mission boards. Paul watched and listened and pondered, convinced that the Army's failure to encourage self-support, even though this choice might have been fostered by sympathy for Korea's post-war plight, snatched away the dignity of a proud and self-reliant part of God's kingdom. No one seemed to understand that Korean Salvationists wanted to be self-sufficient and stood willing, even eager, to endure considerable sacrifice to reach such a goal. One conversation underscored the truth of this for Paul, who had taken his cadet brigade to a country corps. After the day's adventures, he sat with the local officers sipping barley tea and discussing issues.

"We have times," one said, "when we don't get our allowance, and I know that some officers count all the missed months when time comes for the Thanksgiving Offering."

The Thanksgiving Offering this officer referred to was a major one in all of Korea's part of Christendom. Some churches called it a harvest festival, but all churches, including Salvation Army corps, celebrated God's bounty in the autumn, and all believers gave, whether it was money, produce from their small farms, or offspring of their rabbits and chickens.

The man warmed his hands around his tea cup and continued: "My wife and I decided that if God kept us during the year, we would give to meet the needs of the corps and take nothing from the offering for ourselves to make up missed allowances."

Paul pondered the words and the dedication of his fellow officer long after they finished their barley tea and went on their way. Too poor to do anything? Never reach self-support? He didn't buy it. Couldn't, because here was living, breathing proof that the Holy Spirit called the poor as well as the rich to sacrifice, to the dedication of their resources in the service of the Almighty.

It seemed clear that the world's outpouring of concern for Korea, evidenced by tons of relief goods and food commodities plus millions of dollars, blunted the thinking of many, expatriates and Koreans alike, who dealt day by heart-crushing day with the social ills, with the poverty and sickness and death that blighted the nation following the war. To think about self-support and growth for the shabby little churches tucked away among Korea's granite mountains seemed sheer idiocy. Paul often talked with his friend and fellow Asburian, OMS missionary Everett Hunt, about the effect, positive and negative, generated by the huge role that social welfare, its funds, personnel, and ethics, played in the Christian community and beyond.

A major part of what troubled both Paul and Kay in The Salvation Army's stagnation in Korea was the attrition of other expatriate officers who were perceived as unneeded. Might this downsizing affect them as well? Before God the Raders wanted to, felt called to, stay. They wanted to be part of the solution for the problem that burdened their hearts, and their Korean comrades knew this.

Peter Chang tells his impression: "They were clear in their expression that they were in Korea for a long time to come. It was plain they had not come, as some others had, just as a stopover before their next move. Paul and Kay made it very clear that they had a special call from the Lord to serve in Korea."

The Raders spent hours talking over the issues, and Kay read some of the books that fired Paul's soul with hope. Paul wrote to California for literature and a catalog from the Fuller Institute of Church Growth.

Then Kay fell ill. Chronic fever and weakness in her legs remained undiagnosed for weeks. Local doctors couldn't seem to identify the problem. Was it dengue fever? Not sure. Emotional depression followed hard on the heels of Kay's physical disabilities. Finally her doctors recommended she get out of Seoul for a time, a maneuver made possible by adoption agencies who gave orphan escorts free airline tickets in exchange for accompanying four or five babies to their new homes. As a last resort, she tried that. After all, the Raders had been in Korea for ten years with only one five-month furlough back in the United States, not much of a respite from the pressures under which they lived.

The fact that Kay's problems arose in the midst of the decision-making process about Paul's possible study at the church growth institute then got them wondering whether the whole family should take a break and plan some time at home as they worked on the possibility of Paul's pursuit of a doctor of missiology degree at Fuller. While they talked and prayed and wondered, in 1970 Paul sent up a trial balloon by applying to Fuller to see if he could get in. Maybe he remembered the "failure fright" that plagued him and Kay for a few hours back at Southern Baptist Theological Seminary in Louisville. The study opportunities at Fuller looked exactly like what Paul needed and wanted, for not only was he grappling with Army growth problems in Korea, but he had grown hungry for the stimulation of study, a need as natural for him as thirst.

Not everyone in the West can understand this hunger, but for Koreans, a society heavily influenced by Confucian philosophy, it is meat and drink, opening the doors to mental stimulation, not to mention the highest echelons of clout, dignity, and respect. As Commissioner Chang so delicately phrases it, "In my young and immature thinking, it seemed to me that some overseas officers could have been better prepared academically as well as in their ministry prior to their arrival in Korea. But in the case of Paul and Kay, both had graduated from college, and Paul was definitely well prepared for the task since he was a graduate of a theological seminary, even having achieved a Master's in Theology in his studies."

But Chang was not lopsided in his enthusiasm over academic achievement. He writes further, "On the same score, generally when we saw someone well prepared in the academic aspects, somehow they seemed lacking in spiritual dynamics, but both Paul and Kay were well balanced academically as well as in their spiritual enthusiasm and passion for evangelism."

Judging this study project to be right for Paul and impelled by the same nudges of the Holy Spirit that sent him into two other areas of useful study, one pivotal question confronted the Raders: How do we negotiate this?

In those days The Salvation Army did not encourage what might be considered excessive amounts of graduate study, expecting that a burning heart for lost humanity and a respectable knowledge of biblical truth should enable one to point seekers to the Savior. This stance guaranteed some administrative hindrances to Paul's visionary conviction that Fuller's Institute of Church Growth held the answers to Army problems in Korea and that he should spend some time digging out those answers.

As soon as the children finished the school year in 1971, the

Rader family left for their regulation stateside furlough of four months, hoping after they reached the United States to extend it to a two-year study leave. The first item on the agenda when they reached the Eastern Territorial Headquarters in New York, their home base, was to talk to some of the leaders there. Paul petitioned for a two-year study leave, going first to Field Secretary Colonel John Waldron, who thought it was a good idea. However, highly regarded Education Secretary Colonel Margaret Hale didn't like the idea of pursuing studies at Fuller's School of World Missions at all.

"What can California give them that New York cannot?" she questioned.

But Paul, having done his homework meticulously, knew the Fuller program was on the cutting edge, was pioneering in the area of his greatest need. Finally, Commissioner Paul Carlson, who commanded the Eastern USA Territory, told Paul, "We cannot agree to your going to Fuller." He offered the Raders instead a corps appointment, one of the better appointments in the East, it was hinted. But the Raders knew they could not take a full-time corps appointment and at the same time do doctoral studies within two years, and they were unwilling to prolong their absence from Korea.

"Colonel Waldron, please do not tell us what the appointment is," Paul petitioned. "I have no desire to refuse an appointment. Please know that what we're looking for is the opportunity to put together the tools we need to address the unique challenges of Korea. We've given 10 years to Korea and are willing to continue to serve there."

Paul was unshakably convinced that in order to serve profitably in Korea in line with the direction of the Holy Spirit, he must gain the tools of understanding available at Fuller seminary. So he offered that they would go out on their own, take a leave of absence, and assume financial responsibility for his degree program and their family.

The commissioner didn't budge. "You must either accept this appointment or go on 'without appointment' status for a year, which protects your officership," he said.

Physically and emotionally spent, Kay spiraled into deeper depression, hurt, and confused by the haggling over their request. Couldn't they see how important this study is for Korea? Why don't they just agree and let them go? All five Raders went to Georgia and the welcoming arms of Kay's family. Here Kay and Paul thought and prayed and appealed to their leaders in New York once again. And once again they were turned down.

What to do? They decided at last that Paul would go alone to California and begin his studies. Kay's mother, Miss Edith, offered a hospitable and practical solution: "Kay, you come home to us with the children. Let Paul go on out to California. We'll see if we can find some kind of job for you here."

The "without appointment" status suggested by the Commissioner may have protected the Raders' officership, but it stripped them of Army allowance and benefits, so a job for Kay, troubled as she was, became crucial to their financial survival. God did not abandon His obedient warriors, however, and in a miracle maneuver provided a teaching post for Kay in her hometown, this at the end of summer when the school doors were open, the lights on, and all teachers in place—except one for the fourth grade.

At the same time, with an indescribable heart wrench, Captain Paul bid his family good-bye and boarded an airplane for Los Angeles, obedient to his heavenly vision in spite of the cost. He had to wonder what was to become of them all and their affiliation with The Salvation Army even as he marched ahead along a pioneer path whose value few recognized.

Shortly after Paul registered and settled into his work, a postcard photo of the new class, only the second to pursue doctor of missiology degrees there, was published by the seminary. Prominent amongst the sport shirts and sandals stood Captain Rader in uniform. Paul sent one to his Eastern Territorial Commander, Commissioner Paul Carlson, and Carlson said that the sight of Rader in his uniform amongst the other more casually dressed students "convinced him that Paul was truly committed to The Salvation Army."

One wonders if the sight of one of theirs among the scholars and church planters stirred some of the higher ranking Army administrators to go on record that the Raders should be saved for the future, because a variety of voices rose in protest. Colonel Ray Gabrielsen, among others, registered his feelings from his post in Chicago.

"Here's a dedicated couple wanting to help the Army grow, giving their lives to Korea and we're throwing them out? Can these officers be allowed to walk away? You can't be serious!" Not everyone spoke so bluntly, but several made similar points.

Rader contacted the local Salvation Army in Pasadena and Territorial Headquarters immediately upon his arrival. He was still an officer, after all, even though one without appointment. Given his Rader family history and the path he and Kay had followed into the Army and on through their missionary service in Korea, his loyalty to God and the Army remained fixed. He would do what was right, regardless. His situation became known throughout the ranks, and other Rader advocates began to phone Territorial Headquarters people to register their concerns.

One wonders if the upheaval and spirit of revolution fostered in the 1960s contributed to these events. Even though they did not buy into all the headlong changes that took place then, Paul and Kay were in touch with what was convulsing the world's value systems and thought processes. One thing they both believed in that may have been drawn from those revolutionary times was that persons required consideration along with institutions. God-given identities deserved protection.

Before this crisis, Paul highlighted a passage in General Clarence Wiseman's autobiography, *A Burning in My Bones,* that turned out to be relevant to this pivotal moment in Rader ministry:

> The grace of flexibility without surrender of essentials is a gift of the Spirit, a pragmatism firmly bound within the unchanging truth of the founding beliefs, purposes, and passions that have made us what the Lord set us out to be. This sensitive flexibility will prevail so long as the unfettered wind of the Spirit is allowed to blow through us. Openness to the Spirit is more creative than shallow dogmatisms that try to put up the shutters when God seeks to reveal a new thing (192).

So here were personal commitment and conviction of the leadership of the Holy Spirit in conflict with careful, go-by-the-book organizational administrators. Few realized then that the Lord had given Paul Rader a prophetic prescience, the forward-focused ability and willingness to catch a wave of the Holy Spirit's instigation like an experienced surfer who rides the mammoth roller ahead of where it breaks, not paddling along behind it after it's already passed through.

Just a short time into the fall term, Colonel Rice, Western Territory Field Secretary for Personnel, called Paul from San Francisco, saying that Commissioner Paul Kaiser, Territorial Commander, wished to talk. "You fly up—we'll pay," Rice said. Rader responded promptly.

When Paul entered the Commissioner's office, Kaiser pulled his chair from behind his desk in order to sit face to face and converse with his visitor.

"You tell me your perspective of this whole story. I want to hear it."

Paul told his story; Kaiser reacted by suggesting that he take an appointment there in California and study on the side.

"But, sir," Paul explained, "I really feel I need to pursue this full time in order to go back to Korea. Kay and I are both proficient in the language. To stretch this study out for three or four years, we could lose our way, lose connection. This is about our mission in Korea. That's why I'm here. That's what I'm studying about, what I'm working on."

In the end Commissioner Kaiser agreed. "All right. Here's what we'll do. On weekends you can go out and encourage self-denial and mission giving—as a missionary at large."

Kaiser also had an appointment for Kay, a separate one, to work with the youth of the Pasadena corps, which meant she had to extricate herself from her teaching contract in Georgia and move with their three children to California. This resolution of their conflict of purpose with The Salvation Army, rather than easing matters, exacerbated the frustration that Kay suppressed within herself. She shared her conflicts with no one, dragging through preparation for the journey from Georgia to California and the disentanglement from her fourth graders who by now she was enjoying thoroughly. Their tears and howls of protest at her departure cut her to the bone, as did the abandonment of her newborn dream that had materialized into plans to begin work on a master's degree of her own while in Georgia.

Kay ended up resenting the resolution of their status with The Salvation Army rather than rejoicing, as she knew she should. She felt used and abused, still deeply bothered that the Eastern Territory, home turf of all the Raders, had let them walk away rather than working with them on a solution. On the other hand, she knew the East had decided to pay Paul's tuition at Fuller while the West gave them their appointments, which provided the income that enabled them to survive financially while Paul studied full time. But after all the haggling, this gave her only mild comfort. Her greatest joy was knowing that she, Paul, and the children would be reunited after a long nine-month separation. Then to add one more bitter draught to the mix, soon after Kay and the children arrived in California and began feeling their way into new schools and work, Paul departed for Korea for two months of research-gathering for his doctoral dissertation.

On the plus side, Kay plunged into and thoroughly enjoyed her work at the Pasadena corps, for young people always brought her satisfaction. She didn't have to fake her love for her young charges, and as an associate corps officer with responsibility for youth and children, she soon had things humming, things like singing companies, sports, drama programs, choral readings, and day camps. But within her divided heart, concealed by a smiling face and the expected behavior of a willing servant, her resentment over their treatment at the hands of The Salvation Army remained. She spent a year and a half in Pasadena, but within her wounded heart she found little room for forgiveness. Her unresolved problems lay buried, plastered over by professionalism and the proper assumption of duties.

Kay's unfeigned love for children and youth did balance and compensate to a degree her feelings about the Army and their treatment of her husband and thereby her as well. Meanwhile, Paul combined his studies with mission-promoting visits to all the corps in the division, initiating friendships that would come into play in years to come. And Kay, it turned out, was the one of the pair who alone brought corps experience to their team ministry, and everyone who knew what she achieved among the kids of Pasadena saw it as a successful and positive experience, for the pain and anger with which she grappled remained hidden.

Regardless of what was going on beneath the surface of Major Kay Rader's public demeanor (promoted in 1972), both she and Paul maintained unswerving commitment to God's plan for their lives and ministry and to their officer training work in Korea, unaware that a crisis of eternal magnitude was bearing down upon them, that Kay and the Holy Spirit were heading toward an encounter that would transform the way she viewed God's world and her place in it.

7

"This Is It!"

THE PHONE SHRILLED in the summer dusk as Paul set the suitcases by the door, ready for departure in the morning. Kay picked up the receiver. It was Territorial Headquarters calling.

"We've just heard from Korea. Sorry, but your Seoul quarters are not available. Captain Irene Davis is still living there and can't get out for a couple of weeks. Can you stay where you are for that much time?"

Quick-witted Kay replied, "No, we *can't* stay where we are. My successor is waiting to come into this house even as we speak, a widow with four children. How about Hawaii?"

She explained her thinking. "We're routed that way already. Since it's summertime, the camp's in session, and I know one house there has a porch area that will accommodate a family like ours. What do you think?"

"We'll check it out and call you back."

The phone rang again within the hour. "That's a great idea!" came the hearty reply tinged with relief. "Let's do it!"

And so with graduation over, a 358-page dissertation completed, a doctor of missiology degree in hand—plus hundreds of Pasadena young people aware in new ways of God's love and dozens of Salvation Army corps stimulated to participate in the Great Commission—all five Raders flew off to a two-week hiatus in Hawaii. They needed this serendipity, as their heavenly Father well knew, and when the two weeks ended they arrived in Seoul refreshed in mind and body.

Reality set in with a thump, however, as soon as they stepped off the plane in Seoul, still sun-tanned and relaxed. The first thing they discovered was that their car had been sold, the one paid for by Kay's personal friends and family members after

Paul's motorcycle accident. Once again they had to depend on public transportation and sidewalks.

Major Paul Rader was now to take responsibility for the officer training program as principal; Major Kay Rader received no appointment other than "wife of the training principal." Usually in The Salvation Army when a male officer receives an appointment to an administrative post, his wife, of equal rank, takes on the feminine side of the effort with a suitable title and job description. In Korea, however, no definition or structure existed for the wife of the training principal. They did work together some at the college, but Kay held no responsibility of her own for specific areas of work or ministry, a turn of events that aggravated her problems with the Army and her role—or lack thereof—in it.

The following spring, in 1974, Paul went to the Army's International Training Principal's Conference in England. Kay's unresolved bitterness continued to fester behind the facade of her daily routine. Along with the unresolved resentment came more physical problems, thyroiditis this time, although it remained undiagnosed for weeks. Matters slid from bad to worse as Kay sank into depression over her difficulties and her lack of help for them. She may have talked over the problems occasionally with friends she trusted, but no one offered a viable way out.

As she went through various tests under missionary doctors' guidance, Kay suspected they were looking for malignancy, although no one came out and said so. "I was building things up in my mind and was just frantic, really," is how she describes her situation. At the same time she sought to disguise her anguish and appear on the outside as a Salvation Army officer should, a task that loomed harder and heavier with each day's passing.

Korea, like the rest of the world, struggled with an oil crisis during those days, and the Rader quarters was heated with fuel oil. But no oil was available for their heat during a colder-than-normal late winter and on into spring. While Paul was in England at the training principal's conference, Kay took on the battle with the oil company, trying to rectify the shortage. But it couldn't be done, not even by the formidable Kay Rader. She gave up on the furnace and used two electric heaters, one upstairs and one down, and the icy cold aggravated her physical problems.

"So I struggled with the problem of heat, with no car, and no job to do—just a lot of things," Kay reminisces. "The devil knows how to pile it up."

Edie, now a teenager, almost joined the wrong crowd of her peers but by God's grace veered off from that and toward a youth group at the International Baptist church, plus musicals and drama at school where she excelled. J. P., six feet tall at age 13 and the object of pursuit by several girls, played varsity sports even though he was just a middle school student. Fortunately for them all, Jennie was still a little girl, tow-headed and tractable, with an array of friends all over town.

"This was a time when I felt our kids needed someone to be really stable spiritually, but I did not feel stable myself," Kay acknowledges. "I was angry with God. I had not resolved that anger. There was bitterness in me about some things."

What things?

"It may even have gone back to the language study thing, the discrimination and inequity. Then a little prayer card circulated in the Eastern Territory at one point that pictured Paul standing *alone* with his books and urged 'Pray for this missionary.' I was hurt by that and didn't resolve it as I should have. I was having problems, and so I blamed it on that—no one was praying for *me*. I began to feel that nobody cared about me."

Matters didn't stop there, for Satan did indeed "pile it on." Paul's next appointment, increasing his responsibilities and opportunities just a year after their return to Korea, was as Education Secretary, this time with no appointment whatsoever for Kay. This convinced her that nobody cared. "Why am I in this organization?" she wondered. "Why should I even stay?"

Kay began to allow herself to think in such terms. "Maybe this was not God's call to me after all. Maybe he called Paul but not me."

The Fullers' beloved and encouraged little Frances Kay, intimidated by few of the oughts and shoulds of her time, who took it upon herself to correct the manners of evangelist guests, who sent her scholar husband back to the grad school office to point out administrative errors, who shouldered the challenges of homemaking, child raising, language learning, and teaching, was desperate for more personal opportunities to work, to learn, to set things right.

Because of her drive, the scope of her skills, Kay's perception of being ignored, bypassed, and overlooked ignited within her hot anger and resentment, which her spiritual resources at that time did not equip her to deal with.

How can I continue without some evidence of organizational concern for me as a person in my own right? she wondered. Was she not called by God to mission in the same way as her husband? As long as she functioned as an extension or appendage to Paul, she knew she could probably soldier on, but at that time Kay was reading the women's liberation authors and felt herself leaning toward their philosophy. "I wanted to be someone myself. Some of this is part of me, I think, from birth, and part of it then came from a succession of events that intensified as it went along."

One such event was the Raders' two years in the states. "I managed to keep body, mind, soul, and family together for seven months," Kay says. "I went back to teaching school, and I thought 'I can do this!' Nobody there in my school in Georgia cared whether or not I was married. I was just me. So I knew I could stand alone.

"Then in California it was the same. We were not appointed together, Paul and I. Yet when we returned together to Korea, there was no slot for me as a person. That started to niggle underneath, and I let it—which was my mistake, to allow the devil to get into my heart garden and mess up the whole thing. No longer could I smell the flowers."

Kay's depression deepened, partly because of the thyroiditis and partly because of her spiritual "un-grace," a term she uses to describe her state at the time. She drifted along unrelieved, but at the same time God did not ignore His hurting child. Free of any obligation to The Salvation Army and anxious to utilize her time, Kay went over to the Campus Crusade for Christ headquarters in Seoul and offered her services there to Crusade staffers and friends

Nils Becker and Bob Goette. Preparations for Explo 74, a gigantic evangelism effort fielded by Crusade, were underway, and thousands of young people from overseas poured into Korea, creating logistical nightmares for the local staff. These people needed orientation to the city of Seoul, to Korea and its ways. This Kay could handle. She helped set up their orientation program for the United States staff people, teaching them and taking groups of the newcomers on walks to familiarize them with markets, schools, customs. She took charge of providing housing for about 40 of them.

Here I began to see something. Until now one of the reasons I didn't deal with these issues is that I felt I was a professional Christian, a missionary, reluctant maybe, but 12 years into it. Just before Explo I sat through the Brengle Holiness Seminar unscathed. After all, I knew all about that.

But God really pricked me by the attitudes of the kids who came for Explo. They were junior to me by decades, some of them, and yet they seemed to have a deeper understanding of dying to self and surrendering to God's will than I did. They never complained, and I did nothing *but* complain.

There was lots going on then in my heart. Outwardly I looked fine—the plastic smile, the look, trying to keep up a good front with clenched teeth—but no real surrender to whatever God said that might entail humbling oneself.

Admit you're this way? Never!

This unwillingness to submit to the Lord built up within Kay until, she says, "it almost consumed me." Friends could see the conflict and misery written across her face in spite of her professional Christian smile.

On Saturday night, August 17, 1974, during one of the huge evening gatherings of Explo 74, Kay talked with her missionary doctor friend and counselor, complaining, as she remembers it, about not understanding and therefore resenting a long list of flaws and faults.

"I think, Kay," he cut in, "that some of these things are more imagined than real." This, predictably, made Kay angry, but he didn't quit. "I think you need to apply some 220 voltage to your life. Galatians 2:20."

His cryptic comment got her attention. What did he mean? After the Explo meeting with its singing, praying, and preaching, with masses of people in attendance, Kay and Paul made their way toward home through Seoul's jammed streets. Kay fell silent, struck dumb. "I was like a paralyzed person sitting there."

As the family went into the house, Kay told the others, "I want to stay down here for a while." Paul and the children climbed the stairs and left Kay alone in the living room.

"I sat down and opened my Bible to Gal. 2:20 and read it for the first time in a long while."

I have been crucified with Christ and I no longer live, but Christ lives in me. The life I live in the body, I live by faith in the Son of God, who loved me and gave himself for me.

As she read, Kay's thoughts turned to Elizabeth Newbold, one of the persons Campus Crusade invited to participate in training for Explo 74. She and Kay became friends, and Kay confided to Elizabeth some of the difficulties she battled against, how those problems affected her marriage along with all the other parts of her life. Kay told Elizabeth how she felt walled in, unable to control her circumstances, how she felt her whole world threatened to collapse around her.

Rather than commiserate with Kay, however, Elizabeth said to her, "This is something you must work out with God. You're married to Paul Rader, you know, and you're a Salvation Army officer. Find God's solution for your difficulties within that."

Kay disliked the older woman's suggestions. "What do *you* know?" she railed silently from behind her professional Christian's smile. "All you do is flit around the world in your beautiful clothes." But in her heart Kay knew Elizabeth was right—that was the worst part—and couldn't help respecting her for saying it. She knew she didn't want to leave Paul or The Salvation Army, because that's what he loved, and she loved him. God had brought them together—this she knew. And God had called her, as He had Paul, to service as officers in the Army.

So with Elizabeth Newbold's words reverberating in her head and Gal. 2:20 open before her, that Saturday night in the living room Kay looked up and saw Jesus crucified, submitting to the

Cross for her sake. "It was the first time in my life that I realized I also had to be up there with Him. Crucifixion of self. This meant so much, because 'self' for me meant bad attitude, bitterness, rebellion, iconoclasm. I was committed to so many things like this.

"Also I remembered that Jesus humbled himself when He went to the Cross. So I knew I had to overtly, decisively say, 'OK. All right. You win.' It came together for me in three words: *This is it*. And I did it."

"This is it" meant that Frances Kay walked up to the Cross, took a long heartbreaking look at her Savior bleeding and dying there, acknowledged her need to share in His death—and died. Died to hurts, slights, mistreatments. To forcing things to go the way she chose by the set of her jaw, the strength of her hands, the power and logic of her arguments.

Liberation, emancipation flooded in as Kay's commitments to her own agenda dissolved and drained away. The dark lifted, and walls no longer closed her in. She realized in an instant that God knew everything in her heart. She needed no long prayers. Her "This is it" surrender set her free and enabled her. Just like that He came, and her tears flowed.

Then Kay ran upstairs to Paul to beg his forgiveness. Blinded, perhaps, by love and his respect for Kay, he wasn't sure what needed forgiving. Paul did know Kay struggled with a sense of being boxed in by parts of what it meant to be an officer. She had often expressed herself as uncomfortable with the Army covenant that all officers are required to sign, since her role was ill defined: "I give myself to God, and here and now bring myself to Him in a solemn Covenant. I will love, trust and serve Him supremely so long as I live. I will live to win souls, and I will not permit anything to turn me aside from seeking their Salvation as the first great purpose of my life. I will be true to The Salvation Army, and the principles represented by its Flag under which I make this Life Covenant. Done, in the strength of my dear Savior."

Paul also knew, though he never mentioned it, that at times the cold dark presence of Kay's depression surrounded her, emanated from her, and lay its touch on his own spirit. "It would lift then for a time," he remembers, "but would come again. Random comments she normally absorbed without problem would bring it on sometimes."

Paul did not feel that Kay wasn't right with the Lord. Notoriously positive in every situation, he claimed she was "just in a difficult patch." Unwilling to judge, he would not have agreed that Kay was struggling spiritually. After Kay's "emancipation," though, he did write to his parents that Kay had "entered into the most marvelous experience of the fullness of the Holy Spirit. It has been absolutely life-changing for her and has affected our whole family life."

Hearing her parents' voices that Saturday night and sensing an uncommonly emotional atmosphere, Edie burst out of her room and saw her mother's tears. "What's the matter, Mom?"

"I'm not sure I can tell you, but I promise nothing will be the same."

Edie absorbed the fact of her mother's cataclysmic encounter with God and cut straight to what she saw as the heart of the matter. "What about all your women's lib stuff?"

"Well, Edie, right now *I am* the world's most liberated woman," came Kay's beaming reply.

Kay's tears that started to flow when she handed control over to her Lord didn't dry up for two weeks. "The power of the Holy Spirit came over her as she remembered and wrote and wept," Paul says. "It was evident to everyone in our family that something powerful and deep was happening."

With the onset of Kay's liberation, her depression disappeared. She found joy in what she was doing, with or without an appointment from The Salvation Army. She did not try to hide her transformation or the negative factors that led up to it, and when she told her story in the officers' council, Paul says it had an "electric effect."

What happened that night between God and Kay changed not only the focus and tone and aim of Kay's life, but that of the whole Rader family as well. How?

Kay promised her children she would be a better mother, and the five of them, parents and children alike, discovered new unanimity, stronger solidarity amongst themselves.

Jennie, then nine years old, remembers knowing that things were not right at home before that August night, so she listened when her mother promised that things would be different. She watched as Kay handed over to Paul the management of their meager financial affairs and as they became partners in disciplining her and her siblings, in making decisions about what they did and did not do. Their shared authority not only spelled out the parameters of their behavior but increased security and understanding of who and what they were.

Kay's spiritual disciplines took on new vitality, for they were crucial to her well-being, and she finally felt truly qualified to help with the problems with which Edie and J. P grappled each day. Until that Saturday night in 1974, although Kay made decisions quickly and confidently, deep in her heart she didn't feel she had the right to guide and correct, since things were not worked out properly between her and the Lord. In spite of her good front, the Holy Spirit's power never reached her heart.

But now, when Jennie came down the stairs in the morning to the sight of her mother reading the Word or at prayer, she whispered in her little-girl heart, "That's what I want to be when I grow up. And I want my children to see me like that, talking to God."

Without her long look at the Cross, Kay would not have supported Paul in his hard-won opportunity to see Salvationism strengthen and spread across Korea, nor would they have learned how to synchronize their ministry and work together as they did from then on. Before, she had pulled away from Paul. She didn't want to be around him or the Army. "I used to cover my eyes on the way to the kitchen when I passed a pair of Army figurines on the desk. They reminded me of my covenant. It was difficult to train cadets and urge young people toward commitment when I was pulling away from mine. Somewhere along the way before long I would've said, 'I quit!'"

Utopia did not move in on Monday morning, however. Kay still received no appointment, but no matter. She moved through her days bathed in the ecstasy of her encounter as God poured himself into her. She spent unprecedented blocks of time with Him, writing down Bible verses He brought to her mind. Verses learned at college came flooding back. Sometimes as she stood at the sink washing dishes, her joy threatened to overwhelm her. Salty tears mixed with the soapsuds. She found herself loving people she had heartily disliked; she had grown weary of associating with Koreans, but now she loved them.

And then it came—an appointment, as Acting Territorial Home League Secretary, God's way of underscoring that something had indeed happened to Kay Rader. This appointment was unique in many ways. She was to serve under the direction of a Korean officer, Mrs. Commissioner Chun Yongsup, as wife of the first Korean officer to serve as Territorial Commander, with the rank of Commissioner, was apointed Territorial President of Women's Organizations. She quickly took to claiming the rank of a Commissioner without including the prescribed "Mrs.," anticipating, perhaps, long-in-the-future changes in the rank system for women. Commissioner Lee Song-jo, as she now referred to herself, chose to give Kay little or nothing to do, no particular assignment. She had a desk at which to sit and was expected to do so daily, but no real responsibility.

This went on for two years, a hard assignment for Kay in God's school for patience training. Then, at times Mrs. Chun required Kay to travel with her to other divisions in Korea, where she learned much about the lives of the officers plus advanced lessons on patience and submission. She spoke to the women occasionally, served and listened to Mrs. Chun, and waited with fortitude to see what the Lord held in escrow for her.

1. Paul speaking as 15th General at announcement of High Council election result, July 1994.
2. The Raders welcomed back in Los Angeles, Kay still in Commissioner's uniform.
3. Paul and Kay with the Rader brothers in London. *From left,* Lt. Colonels Herb, Damon, and Lyell.
4. The Raders welcomed at International Headquarters in London by, *from left,* United Kingdom territorial leaders, Commissioner Dinsdale Pender and Mrs. Commissioner Winifred Pender; and the Chief of the Staff, Commissioner Earle Maxwell and Mrs. Commissioner Wilma Maxwell.

1. Paul with young amputee at Pediatric Hospital, St. Petersburg, Russia, 1993.
2. Kay with children at Army Girls' Home, Bandung, Indonesia, May 1993.
3. Paul surveys earthquake damage in San Francisco with Billy Graham, 1989.

4. *From left,* Lt. Col. Check Yee and Paul dedicate school in China rebuilt by Army following devastating earthquake, 1990.
5. Paul and Kay with Billy Graham at the National Advisory Organizations Conference in Washington, D.C., 1992

1. Captain Paul preaching in open air in Seoul, 1960s.
2. *Right,* Captain Kay with corps officers: *From left,* Lieutenants Pak Chae-taek and, *center,* Chung Chung-sook, at Sillim Dong refugee settlement area, a cadet field training site.
3. The General enrolls Brazilian soldiers, some of the "Million Marching," 1998.
4. Prayer of bold faith for growth in Korea at 1982 Growth Strategy Conference.

1. Paul and Kay with President Kim Dae-jung after awarding of Order of Diplomatic Service, Kwang Hwa Medal, at the Blue House, Seoul, in 1999. Son, J. P., and his wife, Helen, are seen following.

2. Major Paul translating for General Clarence Wiseman.

3. *From left,* Lt. Colonel Kay reviews program with Mrs. General Maire Wahlstrom, General Wahlstrom; and, *standing,* Major (later Commissioner) Peter H. Chang, 1983.

4. With Lt. Colonel Royston Bartlett, aide-de-camp to the General, at reception celebrating award of presidential medal.

5. Kay teaching Korean cadets.

8

"To Build a Fire"

FROM THE TIME OF THEIR RETURN from the United States, it seemed, the Christian community in Seoul opened multiple doors for both Raders to serve in an ever-expanding number of ways. Kay taught Bible at Seoul Foreign School and also served on its board for a significant length of time. For Christian Women's Club she led Bible classes for a multi-ethnic group of 30 or so women in one of the upscale high-rise apartment buildings sprouting all over Seoul. This ministry spun off opportunities to lead seekers to accept Christ, to disciple women in The Way, and to counsel those for whom life was more than they could handle.

Kay also found herself doing far more public speaking than had been her custom. Various groups within the expatriate community wanted to hear her tell about her life-altering encounter with God during Explo 74. She and Paul together led retreats for other missionary groups. Added to this were her multiplying leadership responsibilities for women's organizations within The Salvation Army. To these she applied creativity, spiritual insight, and drive, the combination of which produced seminars and meetings the likes of which laywomen of the corps and officers alike had never known.

Kay developed a strong sense of the needs of married women officers especially. In a land where men automatically dominate every event and effort, she focused on reminding women and men alike that the women in ministry are called of God, officers in their own right. Major Kay offered institutes for women in every division that bore fruit as she watched them assume the leadership of which they were capable. In every way possible she helped these chosen and trained servants of the Lord to sense their own worth and to strengthen their skills in communicating the gospel.

In the fall of 1974 Paul attended the historic International Congress on World Evangelization at Lausanne, Switzerland, sponsored by the Billy Graham Evangelistic Association. As his commitment to evangelism and his public speaking ability became more widely known, he was invited to contribute to a number of Korea-wide ministries in a variety of capacities, one of which was as part of the volunteer group of pastors who led Seoul Union Church. Most of his daily work was done in Korean, but in the Union Church pulpit he honed his burgeoning preaching skills in English as he and others—Marlin Nelson of World Vision, Presbyterian Sam Moffett, Everett Hunt of OMS, to name a few—rotated responsibilities. He taught church growth/ evangelism seminars interdenominationally—sometimes to crowds in excess of 1,200 people—as part of a team led by Billy Kim, renowned evangelist and Baptist pastor. Other members included Methodist Jack Aebersold, Baptist O. K. Bozeman, and OMS missionaries J. B. and Bette Crouse. They organized and fielded a spate of citywide evangelistic meetings in provincial centers like Chonju, Uijongbu, Taejon, and Kongju, which opened doors for hundreds to convert to Christianity, mobilizing and training numerous believers for more aggressive and effective evangelism on their own.

Paul also served on the founding board of a new graduate school in Seoul designed to help not only Koreans, but scholars from all over Asia, to gain necessary academic degrees in the Asian context without the heavy expense or the temptation to emigrate, both of which seem almost inevitable when two-thirds of the world's college students go to study in the West. The Asian Center for Theological Studies and Mission (ACTS) drew a number of prominent Evangelical leaders from all over the world to teach as visiting professors and lecturers. People like Carl F. H. Henry, Ralph Winter, and Arthur Skevington Wood supplemented the expertise of scholars from numerous mission boards and denominational seminaries in Korea who made up the ACTS faculty.

At the same time, Kay contributed to the work of the drama

committee of the National Council of Churches and served for several years on the Christian Education Committee at Seoul Union Church. Both of them shoehorned into their calendars the soccer and basketball games, the plays and musicals in which their three children inevitably played major roles.

But the work that perhaps gave Major Paul Rader his greatest joy and satisfaction resulted from questions asked by his curious Korean coworkers when he returned, doctorate in hand, from his study at Fuller Theological Seminary. As Commissioner Peter Chang points out, this was "the period when the Army was recuperating from the Korean conflict and, furthermore, when the Army was being rebuilt." It was perhaps "the first time to experience genuine growth based on the religious freedom in Korea of those days, and it was blooming."

Chang points out that a church growth groundswell inundated Korea and "the Army too was aware of the need for drastic growth, yet no one seemed to know how to go about it." Fascinated and curious, Korean officers wanted to know what Paul had learned during his two years away, and they arranged times, a few at first, for Paul to make presentations on church growth. After hearing what he had to say, Paul's friend and fellow Asbury Theological Seminary student Chung Chin-kyung (Paul Chung) made a prophetic remark, "That will open many doors to you." Unknown to either Chung or Rader, those doors already stood ajar, waiting.

The Korean economy took some amazing strides early in the '70s. The business community proved itself capable of hard work and hustle. Major Leonard Grinsted, who was to play a key role in laying the financial groundwork for growth, wrote in *The Officer* that "at the close of the 60s the GNP per capita showed a 200 per cent rise from US$80 in 1960 to $243 in 1970. . . . The eagerness of the Army to expand in Korea stemmed from the realization that this was God's moment to act" (March 1982, 99).

Fueled in part by overseas investment funds, an eager workforce, and a government committed to rebuilding the nation, factories poked their smokestacks into the blue sky. Consumer goods appeared in the shops, and money changed hands. The

women who once sat out in the cold to sell their wares scraped
together enough money to rent stalls in the markets. Tearooms
popped up all across the country, and patrons with adequate
pocket change drank coffee and carried on shouted conversations
over the loud pop music.

And Christians began to pray and to dream of what they
might be able to do in the name of God. In the spirit of the times,
a rising tide of concern within the Army in Korea about church
growth, self-support, and future goals trickled down through the
ranks. They all knew this was what Major Rader had studied in
California and wanted to know what he had discovered, wondering if it had anything to do with them.

Commissioner Chun Young-sup, the first Korean Territorial
Commander, came to leadership with a vision for a vital and growing Army. Throughout the ranks simmered impatience with the status of things, which gave rise to hunger for development and
growth in their various corps and social projects. In an auspicious
convergence of timing and opportunity, Paul in 1975 was appointed Education Secretary, a key leadership role among Koreans giv-
en their reverence for anything related to learning. This afforded
him "a bully pulpit," he calls it, an ideal place from which to function as a catalyst, bringing need and possible solution together. He
began offering church growth seminars in the various divisions;
officers and laypeople attended and participated in what Rader
characterizes as "great times talking about growth."

As he systematically began to visit each division within the
Korea Territory, Rader made sure he pointed out where good
things were happening, things that held promise for significant
future growth. They needed to see what they were doing right, he
knew, because at that time laypeople and officers suffered from
large doses of pessimism that dampened their faith. They knew
all too well that their Army was not keeping pace with the rest of
the Korean church when it came to growth. They had been working hard but had seen few results—hence their frustration.

Paul took to the road usually with a couple of Korean fellow
officers and they traveled either by train or an elderly diesel Land
Rover well acquainted with bumpy, unpaved roads. Their gather-

ings took place in some of the larger corps, occasionally with people sitting on the floor in the old fashioned way, but more often the halls came equipped with benches now that the economy was seeing an upswing. One of the team began the sessions with a devotional, followed by a time of prayer without which no gathering of Korean Christians can take place, it seems. Paul wrote his parents about their first effort: "This has been quite a week! The first three days I spent in Naijang Mountain down in Cholla Puk Do province. We had our first Advance Seminar. All in all, I was quite pleased with the outcome. A good many things went awry, but the Lord was with us, and we learned a lot. I think we will do a better job this week in Taegu."

During the three-day, two-night format he worked out, Rader proceeded from his conviction that his first task was to establish that this was about doing the will of God. "The Army is a vital expression of the Church, the Body of Christ" he told them. "It's a living organism. We're part of the Body, and our task is to see that the Church does grow."

He defined the kind of church he meant. "We want authentic growth, genuine spiritual growth. We want to be bigger, better, and balanced." From this three-point outline that would gladden the heart of any homiletics professor, Paul built his case. He avoided the trap of focusing on numbers alone, affirming that they were talking about Kingdom work, about mission. He sought to allay the fears of these fiercely competitive Koreans that any leader enjoying vast numbers in church would look upon those without them as failures. Don't worry about that, he urged. "What we really want to do is to help the Kingdom grow to fulfill our mission."

After affirming what The Salvation Army was doing right in Korea and aligning its search for growth with God's purposes, Rader then talked to soldiers and officers about how to make it happen. "They loved that part," he notes. Evangelism techniques, church planting strategies, and special community events, of course, figured large in the mechanics of winning nonbelievers to the Savior. So did self-support, that wondrous, frightening concept that collected as many detractors as advocates—at first.

Since 1908, Salvationists in Korea had been schooled in dependency. Whenever the topic of self-support came up, as they looked around at other churches that flourished without denominational or mission subsidy, some veteran officer was sure to say, "No, there's no future in that, because we'll get less money, not more. We'll be lucky if we can keep what we've got." In their view it was like walking off a cliff without a bungee cord, for they were accustomed to lurching along on their slender subsidies from International Headquarters, and the thought of cutting loose from that with no guarantee of anything else was hard to imagine.

Others rose in response to the fear of change, exhibiting remarkable courage as they peered down a path they had not yet walked. "But we have resources," they countered. "If we mobilize them and change our mentality, we can break out. We are committed to seeing the Army establish new corps and watching grow the ones we now have. We'll never do this unless we become self-reliant and develop new resources from within."

As the issue of self-support gained momentum in the struggle against fearful criticism by the opposition, Paul felt no compunction against urging his fellow leaders toward sacrifice, something he knew many of them already practiced. He had seen the little bags of rice carried straight from humble kitchens to waiting receptacles in corps halls, offerings to help those even poorer. He knew that watches and gold rings sometimes showed up in collections when buildings needed expansion or replacement. Now all they needed was to think beyond what had always been and trust God for that which lay outside their earthbound imaginations.

To have for the first time in Army history a Korean as Territorial Commander was God's perfect timing. Commissioner Chun Young-sup and his top administrative officer team now confronted the opportunity, the responsibility to think, to dream, to act upon God's directive to tell His name among the mountains, the rice paddies, the growing cities, and the seaside villages of their land. Self-government was already upon them, and surely they could manage self-support as well, both of which foster self-respect, something that Korea as a nation was gaining daily as she recovered from war's devastation. Paul's Korean officer colleagues believed in this and hammered away at the concepts. And self-support took hold.

During this period a number of corps moved into this realm, voluntarily cutting off their subsidy. This meant no guarantee of officers' salaries. On the other hand, it also meant that some of the larger corps garnered enough on their own to begin to send support, on their own, to smaller ones.

About this time Major Grinsted got the idea to develop an Army-owned patch of ground that fronted a busy Seoul street just a block away from the training college—this from a concept put forth by Commissioner Peter Chang's father (*The Officer,* March 1982, 99-100). Financial Secretary Grinsted suggested a plan that called for the Army to work with Shell Oil Company, where his brother was an executive, to erect a nine-story building on the site where once "social services operated a relief centre and students' hostel in a dilapidated building" (100) with Shell as the major tenant and The Salvation Army as owner; the Army would forego its own use of Shell House for the first decade after its completion. When the deal was consummated—"the 9-story high-class building was fully occupied immediately upon completion" (100)—it generated a helpful amount of revenue, which eventually provided a revolving loan fund for corps development, seed money that encouraged officers with dreams of growth that it might be possible after all.

During those days Paul saw one of his favorite maxims come into play, for he had always said, "The church won't grow until people get angry." Such intensity of feeling comes from reflecting on dreams stifled by focusing too long on counting the cost of growth. Paul suffered no significant opposition to the facts and theories he offered in the seminars, but some who heard him evidenced discomfort—even to the point of red-faced, high-pitched arguments—with change, new ideas, and what they perceived as threats against the status quo. Add to that the implied criticism that what they had done to that point was not good enough, and the whole business hoisted blood pressures over the danger mark more than once.

Unruffled by controversy in the divisional seminars, in 1975 a five-day Growth Strategy Conference convened at a retreat center operated by the women of OMS-founded Korean Holiness Church in Taejon, down in the center of the Korean peninsula. To this were invited choice people with leadership potential—officers and laymen of all ages—and a strategy for new growth within The Salvation Army was laid out before the delegates. Captain Peter Wood, a key player in the event and in implementing the vision thereafter, wrote an article for *The Officer* describing the conference in detail ("Laying Themselves on the Line," November 1982, 483-86). Before the conference closed, those assembled gathered around a large map of Korea with areas marked where they thought it possible to plant new corps in the name of the Master. Together, placing their hands on the map in an act of faith, they asked God to enable them to realize their vision and to guide them, to fill them with discernment and power. The people who prayed over the map of their homeland that day came away gripped with enthusiasm, optimism, and faith, ready to launch a loving assault on the sectors of their nation still unacquainted with their Savior.

Financial Secretary Captain Peter Wood wheedled out of IHQ money generated by the cooperative scheme with Shell Oil Company to set up and manage a revolving loan fund as seed money to open new corps and stimulate growth. This contributed a valuable impetus to the realization of the vision that came out of the Taejon conference. General Wiseman mentions the scheme in his autobiography, *A Burning in My Bones*:

> Before visiting Korea I had heard of the remarkable growth of Christianity in the country. . . . Nevertheless, I got the impression that only the fringes of the population were being touched, and conversations with the Territorial Leader, Commissioner (sic) Chung Yong Sup, and others revealed that this was so. We held a number of discussions about the growth of The Army in Korea, the last one taking place in the airport just prior to our departure. . . . A leading officer suggested that a *revolving fund,* from which loans might be available on reasonable terms, would help new corps that found it difficult to fully finance their first places of worship from local resources.

After negotiations with International Headquarters, the special fund was set up. It is carefully administered so as not to compromise local self-help and to ensure prompt repayment to protect the fund's future viability (250).

Seminars and the loan fund combined to open the eyes of Korean Salvationists—laypeople and officers alike—to the unfettered power of the God they served and to peer into the kit full of tools Major Rader brought back from his study time. Out of the seminars came not only commitment to evangelism and corps growth, but grappling with the need for more officers, with the business of church construction. "We can't possibly" turned into "This might work!" for many of them, and the fire lit among them then still burns today.

That burning connects with a moment that arose between Paul and his older brother, Damon, in their dormitory room at Asbury College. Back in the mid-50s the brothers—one tall and rangy, the other more compact, muscular—took a rare bit of time to talk quietly together. Wanting to affirm Paul, Damon said, "I picture you as a Bible teacher, Paul, an encourager of others."

Of the moment Damon said later, "I never thought of Paul in terms of dynamic leadership. After all, this was my kid brother!"

But Paul turned to look into Damon's eyes and said, "No, sir. I believe God has called me to build a fire in people's bones!"

A moment of passion and declaration is how Damon characterizes what passed between them. "Wonderful" he calls it.

Content that the fire had caught, within a few months Rader received a new appointment, relinquishing that of Education Secretary. In a letter to his parents, by then retired in Ocean Grove, New Jersey, he described what came as "a bolt from the blue. . . . I received a wire from the Chief of the Staff (the General's right-hand man at International Headquarters) yesterday appointing me Assistant Chief Secretary for the territory. I hope you were sitting down when you read that—fortunately, I was!"

Lieutenant Colonel Paul, promoted in 1977, wasn't sure what his new appointment involved but took an educated guess. "It will, of course, involve a great deal of administrative detail and sitting on boards and the like." He knew that part of his job was to link Korea with the international Army. "I have to stay close to the office and keep the mail moving—as well as supporting the TC [territorial commander] and CS [corps secretary] in decisions on all major personnel, program, policy and fiscal matters. . . . It is all very challenging and important, and I am grateful for the opportunities to grapple with the policy concerns that it offers."

Not one to miss an opportunity, he went on to speculate, "It will also provide an opportunity to implement some of my own long-standing goals for the territory. Among them—

1. Double the number of corps and soldiery in next 10 years.
2. Send out 5 missionary couples from the territory.
3. Recruit 2 Western missionary couples and one single from the United States if possible."

Paul closed his letter to his parents, as he always did, by asking that they remember him and his family in prayer.

Both Kay and Paul felt the need for prayer as ministry opportunities tumbled in upon them. Paul spoke and taught in Hong Kong, Japan, and Indonesia, as well as the United States. Kay accompanied a Korean contingent as delegate and translator to London for several weeks at the Army's International College for Officers. In 1980 the World Evangelization Crusade assembled in Seoul, and for five days Kay taught in Korean a daily prayer seminar attended by some 3,000 women, while Paul spoke to international pastors and other professionals. On the invitation of President Dennis Kinlaw, Paul and Kay led student revivals at Asbury College.

As they poured themselves into every opportunity God sent their way, fire burned steadily, brightly among Salvation Army corps across Korea. In three months alone, eight new corps openings took place, and 17 declared themselves ready for self-support. A small country corps "seeded" three others nearby and through this selfless giving found itself growing. The training college strained at its venerable seams with an abundance of cadets. The Westgate Central Corps raised $350,000—from its soldiery—for a new building seating over 500 people. "I doubt any corps in Army history has ever done that—from their own people," Paul wrote his parents.

In the midst of their scorching schedules, Kay and Paul went to Chonju for physical checkups at the Southern Presbyterian hospital. When missionary doctor David Seel listened to Paul explain some of his current symptoms, which he felt sure were nothing remarkable, Seel said, "If you want to be around very long, you better get up and start moving."

Paul had begun a weight loss program in 1975 after reading Stan Mooneyham's *What Do You Say to a Hungry World?* and had lost 40 pounds. A hearty and enthusiastic eater, he had decided to cut back on his intake as he considered the millions who go without an adequate diet. In July of 1975 he told his parents his views on the matter: "I am dieting, for a number of reasons, and am now down to 197, on my way to 185. The Lord has really spoken to me about being even 1 lb. overweight in our kind of world. It's a *personal* thing, though, and I have no desire to tell others what they should do at this point. I only know what he told me."

On the downside of such conscientiousness, some Korean friends, assuming that all meals plus their content and size were Kay's responsibility, asked if she was trying to kill her husband. (Many Asians prefer beefy men with hearty appetites.)

But as he listened to Paul tell about his dizzy spells and how he fell asleep the minute he dropped into his chair for a quiet moment, Seel pointed out that in spite of the lost pounds, the sedentary Paul was not in good shape in terms of exercise. Hence his ominous warning.

So activist, disciplinarian Paul acquired James Fixx's *The Complete Book of Running* and decided to try jogging. He began in the street outside their quarters and the first day "I ran in street shoes," he says. "I ran for about half a block and collapsed." Soon after that inauspicious beginning he rounded up some sneakers, an easy task since by now Korea was shoeing the world. At first he ran at night to avoid embarrassment as he chugged and puffed along the street. Soon, however, the persistent Lieutenant Colonel pushed back the barriers to his fitness program and ventured farther from home, around corners, over hills.

Kay decided to join her husband. "At first I ran 100 paces and then walked 100 paces," she says. "We even went in different

directions at different speeds." Soon, however, the disparity between their running skills narrowed, and they jogged through
Seoul's early-morning traffic side by side. Both had read in one
of their jogging books that "love is running at your partner's
pace." Paul experienced dramatic improvement in his health;
dizzy spells and sleepiness disappeared; they both committed to
a pattern for living that abides.

As the decade of the '70s drew to a close, Paul's letters to his
parents revealed in his understated comments and illegible hand-
writing that fire still burned in the spiritual bones of Korean Salvationists.

October 1979. Spiritual Day at the training college.
Ready response morning and afternoon. The 2nd yr. cadets
on the field (17 of them) came back for the day, and it made a
group of 44 cadets, the largest in 30 yrs. . . .

We opened a new corps at Song Nam . . . on Monday
night. Packed hall. Great excitement. The Yong Dong Po
corps had contributed $10,000 to securing and equipping the
new hall. . . .

September 1980. I'm sending two pictures of Kay's
School of Prayer during 80 WEC. She is preaching tomorrow
night at one of the Evangelical Churches here as a result of
the School of Prayer. . . . Her first one day Home League Mi-
ni Camp was a tremendous success with 256 present. . . . It
was down in a country division.

February 1981. Terr. Growth Strategy Conference, the
27th-30th. There was a marvelous oneness of purpose, clarity
of vision, and intensity of faith as we planned for the future:

Total 200 corps by '83 (our 75th anniv. year!) and 300 by
1990

Total 80 cadets in training by '83

Total 15,000 seekers per year by '83

So praise God for bold faith! . . .

October 1981. We're just home from the dedication of a
new corps building here in Seoul. . . . The building jammed
with people. Shouts of praise and rejoicing. . . . Since they
were unable to get a truck up to the building site, all the ma-

terials had to be lugged up from the road by handcart. . . . They dedicated it debt free without any THQ help. The cost was just under $100,000.

Slipped into the joyous whirlwind of the Raders' lives—the rush of family triumphs and challenges, the incessant invitations to preach and teach—came another dedicatory moment for Paul when he was installed as Korea's Chief Secretary, an appointment bearing heavy responsibility. Kay was in London at the College for Officers, so Paul stood alone as he contemplated what was happening.

"What unusual providence brought Kay and me to this place!" he wrote. And he credited his parents' faithfulness "that these responsibilities have been placed upon us at this early stage."

He then went on to say, "An installation is only a narrow, garlanded doorway into a broad world of responsibility with its steep and lofty heights, swamplands of discouragement, and dark woods of a thousand dangers. We shall have our crosses to bear. But at this point of new departure it is good to feel the love and support of those who care and to know that one is never alone."

It was as if God moved both Raders from apprenticeship to journeyman status in his leadership training program. Responsible for all communication between Korea and London, which entailed translating back and forth between Korean and English, Paul found himself working under and developing sincere respect for the Korean senior officers he served, first Commissioner Kim, Hai-duk and upon his untimely death, Colonel Kim Soonbae. For the next six years Kay acted as the Women's Territorial President in Mrs. Kim's stead because of the older woman's ill health. Kay and her team built up the women's department both in number and forms of outreach. From 1977 to 1983, as each Rader developed leadership skills, the added dimension of working cross-culturally solidified their world view, the ability to envision God's Kingdom without borders, which characterized and colored everything they said and did from then on.

During these years of working, acting, ministering, new challenges for Kay and Paul were forming on the horizon. Radical change would soon draw them away from the land they loved so much and served with such passion. An appointment on the other side of the world would uproot this pair of partners and set in motion a deluge of responsibility and challenge even beyond that which they faced in Korea.

9

Marching Orders

EVEN BEFORE THEY WERE TOLD where and when, the Raders knew an appointment away from Korea was inevitable and approaching fast. Because of this impending change, they spent time together talking over the situations of their three children, trying to assess how such an upheaval would affect them, for their growing-up years, spent in Korea, were hardly those of an average North American family.

Kay remembered when their tow-headed four-year-old son had peered up at his mother, weary with the multitude of strangers named Uncle-this and Grandma-that who were suddenly thrust upon him during his first home leave from Korea, people who beamed at him and crunched him in their arms.

"Is it OK if we don't have hugging?" he queried. "I like hand-shaking instead."

Kay smiled in understanding at her small son, who was going through his first furlough, that missionary institution when one packs up, leaves the appointed country of ministry, and treks back "home," although for many children of missionary families, their home country has no genuine feel of home about it. Consequently, missionary kids (MKs) often are more comfortable in their adopted countries than in the land that gave them passport and nationality. Thus, MKs become third-culture kids. Perhaps not fitting precisely into either the land of their origin nor the place where they live, they form their own culture by overlapping the two that shaped them.

How would a new appointment, a pivot westward, affect the other three members of the Rader family? As they faced their own uprooting from Korea, their home for the past 22 years, Kay

111

and Paul looked back across those years, assessing their effect on their three children. How would Edie Jeanne, James Paul, and Jennifer Kay handle the dissolution of the only home they had ever known? What if the nest they were emptying disappeared entirely? What then?

J.P., the little guy who wearied of hugs from stranger relatives, had grown into a athletic prodigy, playing varsity sports ahead of his time and capturing during high school a shelf full of trophies in soccer, basketball, tennis, and swimming. In spite of spending his junior year living with the Gabrielsens and excelling at basketball in Indiana, where the game reigns and Hoosier Hysteria takes over each spring, his heart remained captive to Korea, and he was preparing to return there to teach, he hoped, in Seoul Foreign School along with his wife, Helen Rehner, herself an MK from Colombia.

Edie, graduated now from Taylor University and with two years of teaching already in her résumé, was newly returned to Korea thanks to a job offer at Seoul Foreign School. Her writing, musical, and dramatic skills came into play each day in her classroom.

Jennie, too, had left Korea for college. Ray Purvis, former Baptist short-term missionary whom she met during high school, loomed large in her life. Matters seemed settled on that score, which the Raders acknowledged with joy and peace.

All three children seemed to be moving into useful, productive, creative lives under the control of the Savior. Their parents knew they had much for which to be thankful.

They were thankful for an excellent school situated in the city of Seoul. They had been spared the emotional tugs and the pitfalls of going off to boarding school.

They were thankful for the positive attitudes evidenced by all three regarding Korea, the United States, The Salvation Army. No bitterness, no resentment, no disabling fear in sight.

They were thankful for surrogate parents in Jeanne and Ted Gabrielsen and in Mary Jim Lester, who had made themselves available to their children and would continue to do so whenever the occasion arose.

They were thankful for all the special opportunities for them to see Venture for Victory athletes play to win against Korea's best teams and then boldly share their faith before crowds of sports fans; to hear Asbury College's Singing Ambassadors in concert in Korea and watch those talented, attractive young people speak of God's grace in their lives; to meet and listen to many of the Evangelical world's most prominent spokespersons.

They were thankful for all the hours spent in family worship time, always punctuated by the irrepressible Edie's insightful and humorous observations, basking together in warmth and love and the Lord's presence.

They were thankful for holidays shared with dear and abiding friends—Korean and Western—knowing that the Lord had placed them in families of His creation in substitution for blood relatives so far away.

Again, J. P. summed it up well when as just a boy he listened to his father preach at Indian Springs Holiness Camp Meeting in Georgia. Paul was talking about God's promise to King David, saying, "I will build you a house."

J. P., child of Salvation Army missionary officers and all that means as far as geography, economics, and impermanence of dwelling are concerned, whispered to his mother, "I'm thinking about what that means to me."

God gives His children houses, shelters not made with hands. And Edie, J.P., and Jennie, moving into adulthood, all knew this loving God intimately and were learning to let Him lead them. For this Kay and Paul were most thankful of all.

Early in 1983 Paul wrote his parents his view of impending changes, acknowledging, "We must expect a change before too long." He cited the upcoming retirement of their Territorial Commander, Colonel Kim Soon-bae, who had been appointed to lead the territory after Commissioner Kim Hai-duk's death. "We have no idea what the future holds. But all indications seem to be we will leave Korea then. Who knows? It might be best for us and for Korea to be gone awhile. Twenty-one years is a fair stay. But please *nothing* definite yet. Only my surmisings and a few hints."

A letter from Chief of the Staff W. Stan Cottrill, written September 7, 1983, came from London on the 19th. He informed the Raders that the General had decided to "make a change of appointment which will involve your return to the U.S.A., almost certainly effective at the 1st January, 1984." He acknowledged their "considerable number of years in Korea" and said that the main purpose of this letter was to inform them of the move and "to help you in your longer term planning and thinking, and notification of your new appointment will reach you directly from the National Commander for the U.S.A."

Later in the autumn, while the Raders were visiting the Army's divisional headquarters in Chunju, a call came for Paul, who moved across the room and picked up the receiver.

"Yoboseyo!" His voice reverberated through the room, more out of habit than from fear of a poor connection.

Kay's heart skipped a beat. "I knew what to expect even as he took the phone," she said later. Paul fell silent after the normal preliminaries necessary for a phone call in Korea. In that moment, forever burned into their memories, they learned that word had come from the United States to territorial headquarters in Seoul that Paul's new appointment was to be principal of the training college in Suffern, New York.

Only a few months remained in Korea. It was a radical shift from his post as Chief Secretary and back into officer training for Paul, a move that at the moment stimulated more questions than answers for him, but being the staunch, loyal Salvationist that he was, he embraced it without flinching.

Edie wept when her parents told her about the phone call. After all, she had been back home in Korea and into her new teaching job only three months and now faced losing the familiar sheltering presence of her parents. Maturity and spiritual stability soon gained the upper hand, however, and she told Paul and Kay, "I'm being selfish. You need this change in your lives. I'm not going to worry you with my feelings."

Helpful, too, was the fact that Jack Moon, fellow Seoul Foreign School teacher and India missionary kid, was spending a noticeable amount of time building a friendship with Edie. His presence around the house offered prescient comfort to Paul and

Kay as they struggled with abandoning their daughter so soon after her return to Korea.

Edie gave her parents that Christmas—just days before they left for the U.S.—a song she wrote that shared with them her heart and attitude. She titled it "A Vision of Love."

> *Lord, I come to You today*
> *And I thank You for the gift of love*
> *You have displayed through these two.*
> > *They took me as a child*
> > *And followed Your will*
> > *In each lesson they taught*
> > *And the advice they brought,*
> > *So that as I grew*
> > *I could see more of You.*
> > > *Father, You've brought them many miles,*
> > > *Seen them through so many trials.*
> > > *But each step of the way*
> > > *Your faithfulness has brought them*
> > > *To their knees in praise.*
> *Leaving their homes behind*
> *They committed their lives as a*
> *Sacrifice to Your will*
> *So that others could feel*
> *Your presence in their lives,*
> *So that others could receive*
> *Your gift of life.*
> *Lord, I know they're in Your hands.*
> *Their lives are a part of Your perfect plan,*
> *For You will guide them.*
> *You'll abide with them*
> *As You enfold them in a*
> > *Vision of love.*

Being of a nature quite different from Paul's, Kay's disengagement from her Korean home was marked by pain and a sense of loss. Her grief was long, strong, and real. She wrote about it finally for the Army's April 1995 issue of *The Officer* magazine. Excerpts from that article allow glimpses into her heart.

"Experience had taught us to anticipate change. . . . But I was not . . . ready for this particular challenge." She knew she was losing Korea and its people, the land to which she had come as a "young officer/wife/mother" and had invested her energies and gifts in the people among whom she lived.

"I dreaded leaving the women of Korea," she wrote. She had "initiated an expansion of women's organizations" and "found working with these energetic, highly motivated women officers both stimulating and exhilarating." Leaving them and the mutual commitment to ministry she felt with them spread a sense of loss across her days as they went through the farewell gatherings in Korea—"not homesickness. This was grief."

Kay was grieving for Paik Ki-hwa, her Korean persona. After her turning point encounter with the Holy Spirit in 1974, opportunities for ministry had poured into her life beyond anything she had previously imagined. Among the Koreans with whom she moved and worked, she was known as Paik Ki-hwa, which translated freely means Cleansed Christian Flower. And now it seemed that Paik Ki-Hwa must be laid to rest, for as Kay knew, in the "Eastern Territory School for Officer Training, no one knew about Paik, Ki-hwa. They did not know she existed." Kay assumed there would be "little demand . . . for the background and experience that enable one to function cross-culturally," and so she felt that the part of her that was called Cleansed Christian Flower "was dying a slow death."

The commitment Kay made to God back in 1974 still governed her life, however, for she was cleansed indeed, and so shoulder to shoulder with Paul, she marched into their next appointment, expecting their Lord to fit them both for whatever service He had planned. If it meant burying Paik Ki-hwa, so be it.

10
1984-1986

PAUL AND KAY RADER headed out into the winter dark for one last early morning run in Seoul. They bundled themselves against the cold, and their breath hung in white puffs as they stretched out protesting muscles that preferred to stay back upstairs in bed. Discipline won over as usual, and they began jogging along the narrow street in front of their home. Quiet for a change, each was reflecting on how very soon they would leave for good this gritty, overcrowded, beloved city.

They ran past a gaggle of women merchants squatting beside the street arranging their wares on straw mats. The women paused in their chatter to gaze at the tall foreigners running by. And as if that were not strange behavior enough, they watched Kay break stride and turn to stare back at them for a long moment. *Who could understand the ways of these big-nosed people? Was she crying? Out here in the street?*

Kay stood and wept, embarrassing, uncontrollable tears streaming down her face. "These are my people!" her heart cried out. "These women need me to be their advocate, to stand in the gap and let it be known that they're worthy."

For Kay, that morning's run was over. Turning on her heel, she dashed for home. They had promised before God to go where sent, to obey orders, and Kay felt the cost of that promise as she acknowledged once again that, to her dismay, Korea was no longer their home, that the rapport built with Korean women—Army officers and laity alike—would no longer be central to her life and ministry.

Paul felt the loss as well, of course. He had enjoyed his Chief Secretary role especially, standing as facilitator and expeditor between the fires of spiritual and numerical growth he had helped to ignite and Army organizational guidelines and stipulations emanating from International Headquarters. He relished supporting his Korean Territorial Commander and reveled in the demands such opportunities placed on him, because every action, every initiative, every word spoken while on the job—for both Paul and Kay—was Korean, not English. But Paul, perhaps inured to change because of his Salvation Army heritage, didn't seem to root as deeply as did Kay; at least he transplanted with less trauma than that felt by his partner.

And now the Eastern Territory School for Officer Training beckoned them back to the United States. Packing was finished, and airline tickets lay with their passports in the drawer. Their installation service in Suffern, New York, was scheduled for February 2, 1984. Time to dry tears, to trust the Lord to care for the people they loved so dearly and for the work among them that had been their life. Time to meet training staff and cadets, to settle into new quarters, to find out which Suffern streets were friendly to maturing joggers. Time to discover God's plan for this appointment and claim His comfort for the pain generated by change.

Their arrival in Suffern was accompanied with ceremonial fanfare and flourish, an Army specialty. A welcome banquet nourished their bodies, and the installation program must have stimulated their souls with its singing and brass band music and the opportunity for each to share what lay on heart and mind at this pivotal moment. At the service of installation, which was conducted by Commissioner Orval Taylor, Paul's proud father, Lieutenant Colonel (retired) Lyell Rader offered the prayer of dedication in a penetrating voice more often used on city streets than in paneled halls.

Paul and Kay responded immediately to the warmth and graciousness extended to them by staff and cadets. Added to this was the singular joy of having Damon and June Rader as part of their team, the first time two branches of the widespread Rader family served together in the same appointment, although Jeanne and Ted Gabrielsen had served in Korea for several years, albeit in another town. Since Damon and June had been part of the training college family for several years in teaching ministry, Damon as director of personnel and June as senior instructor, Paul and Kay frequently drew comfort and insight from them. Paul later team-taught with June and found her to be a unique individual, singularly gifted, with strong insights and a frequently fresh point of view.

Damon remembers those years of working together with his brother as meaningful to him. "It was a very happy thing for me. It gave us an opportunity to get reconnected after all of those years, to talk about some things from our growing-up years. I felt the need to say, 'Forgive me.' We talked about some of those things."

As a teenager, Damon's skills had lain along scientific and engineering lines, while Paul liked books, art, music. Paul was tall and loose-knit, while Damon was compact, muscular, and loved sports. Damon, secure in his special comaraderie with their scientist father—"I was his alter ego," he says—admits that as an adolescent he sometimes enjoyed punching his younger brother's arms and chest and did so without fear of parental reprisal, behavior that troubled him long years later.

The two brothers lunched together on Thursdays while they worked together in Suffern, "making sure we were connected and whatever healing needed to take place did so," Damon says. "Whatever from the past that had negatively impacted him [Paul], he'd already worked through. None of my concerns were well founded."

As Damon watched Paul move into his responsibility as principal, he observed how effective his brother was in a leadership role. "Paul is always superbly prepared. Even in Monday morning assembly he had a carefully prepared statement, a devotional for the cadets . . . like a Sunday morning."

Damon is generous in his admiration for the brother he once liked to pick on. Speaking of Kay and Paul, he says, "They've got poise, charm, elegance . . . something about them that's beautiful. At the same time a commanding presence . . . no bossiness in Paul, no ego trip. He worked beautifully in weekly coordinating council meetings . . . sensitively, with a sense of direction. He worked for consensus. It was a time of harmony, time when we felt proud to be part of the team."

Teamwork, partnership, was becoming the trademark of Paul and Kay's leadership style. In matters great or small they sought to move together toward resolution or innovation, which was no simple task, they knew, because of the disparity of their appointments. As training principal, Paul readily swung into action, but Kay, shorn of her Korean staff, coworkers and specific goals and tasks, was at first not so stretched and challenged as she was in Korea.

Others, however, who watched and worked with the Raders—cadets and coworkers alike—found themselves led into new areas of thought and behavior as they watched their leaders grapple with the business of reentry into North American culture. Paul still burned with a hunger to see church growth spread through The Salvation Army on all its worldwide fronts, the United States included. He held a seminar for the Suffern training staff and taught growth principles to the cadets, all liberally laced with facts and illustrations from his years in Korea. Still lighting fires, he wanted the staff "to catch the vision, to be able to communicate that vision to the cadets."

Assistant Principal Major Ken Baillie recognized that Paul's "aura" was "always one of a leader" and agreed with his emphasis on growth but doubted that the Army in America would take hold of these concepts. "Until our top leadership takes hold of this," he said, "it's not going to happen." He could not know, of course, that he had uttered a prophecy of sorts, for within five years General Eva Burrows convened an International Church Growth Conference to alert the Army in the United States and around the world to its need to take action in this particular arena. General Burrows had studied in depth the teachings on church growth emanating from Fuller Theological Seminary's School of World Mission and encouraged their use within The Salvation Army. (See Henry Gariepy's *General of God's Army,* 139, 195, 321.)

Most people at the training college knew that Paul and Kay grappled with the conspicuous consumption that surrounded them on their return to the West. Sensitized by a hungry, hurting world, they had committed themselves to fitness and to conservative eating habits, and while Paul did not wish to force his feelings on the matter upon others, he and Kay wondered about their responsibility for the institution they were appointed to lead as they watched the daily waste of food from the school dining room. How could they not compare this with what they had seen of poverty and hunger in other parts of the world?

In the light of these concerns, Kay Rader and Joy Baillie, as director and associate director of special services, attended a world hunger conference in search of ways to put well-fed American Salvationists in touch with starving people around the globe. The cadets' missionary fellowship also sponsored an international meal with samples of food, or lack thereof, from all over the world.

Kay and her committee grappled with the waste of food from the dining room. "Take all you want, but want all you take," became their motto as they created displays of wasted food culled from the school's garbage cans. Their efforts were well received for the most part, but some felt that "Mrs. Rader doesn't have to teach us about hunger. We already know." Both Raders were learning that a segment of any group they were appointed to lead and with whom they sought to share their vision would misunderstand and would oppose their innovative goals.

Cadets Jim and Pat LaBossiere watched it all with interest: the Raders' reorientation back into North America, their feelings about United States affluence, and their obvious dismay over the waste of food. "They opened our eyes to our plenty in comparison to the rest of the world," Jim admits. "Some were annoyed by this, while some readily understood how 20 years overseas would affect one's viewpoint."

The Captains LaBossiere look back on the Raders' influence during their cadet days. "The Raders brought understanding of the wider world . . . always international, wide in scope and spectrum." Jim asserts. "Their passion and the understanding of other cultures . . . opened my eyes."

During their time in Suffern, Paul as training principal was assigned to the teaching staff of the Brengle Memorial Holiness Institutes at the School for Officer Training, Central Territory, in Chicago. He enjoyed fielding the questions tossed his way, interacting with his hearers, during these times. He also taught doctrine at the training college, and Pat LaBossiere "felt stretched and intellectually challenged" by his lectures.

She was not alone in this, for in Paul Rader's other classes and special lectures his students found him to be a good and kind teacher, although he required them to write papers and held them up to college level work, "perhaps leaning toward grad school," Pat reckons. "Some in the class were really stretched."

In the eyes of some of those they led and served, Kay and Paul were "obviously equipped by God with special graces and skills," and the LaBossieres found them to be warm and approachable, especially so during and after a local city-sponsored race. Some of the cadets who entered the race found the course confusing and lost their way, but the Raders did their homework, checked out the course, and finished it without error.

Afterward they sat over breakfast in a McDonald's restaurant with Jim LeBossiere and "just talked. It was very personal and we saw beyond the public persons. I appreciated it and know others who had similar experiences did too."

Eugene and Edie Pigford were appointed to the Suffern staff a short time after the Raders, and Eugene says of Paul, "He was both a reader and runner, and cadets and staff alike knew that they would be hard put to best him in either endeavor."

Pigford said, "Paul as training principal set the standard for study and statesmanship from the pulpit and had a positive but no-nonsense approach to his leadership role." He also observed that he "had a backbone as hard as flint when he was defending a principle that was important to him, but he was warm and genuinely concerned for people when they were hurting and vulnerable."

He says that Kay, like her husband, is "an avid reader and thinker. She has always been a gracious, hospitable woman who both exemplifies and advocates the best in women's leadership roles in ministry."

Partnership between Paul and Kay Rader became established during the later years in Korea. They forged between them the belief that "you support each other even when doing separate things," for they knew from experience that "at times even partners function independently, wife or husband."

As Roger Green wrote of The Salvation Army founders in his biography, *Catherine Booth,* "Neither partner begrudged the other time away from the home for the sake of the gospel. There was mutual support throughout their growing ministry for the work that the Lord had laid on them, and their times of separation were made more bearable by long correspondence as well as by their anticipation of being with each other again."

But the business of short separations between husbands and wives for the sake of ministry was only part of the partnership commitment growing up within both Kay and Paul. During their latter years in Korea, when each of them carried heavy responsibility, they advocated and aided in the growth of solidarity and equality, especially among married women officers who were called into ministry just as clearly and personally as their husbands.

Convinced that this was God's plan for the unique part of His Church called The Salvation Army and anxious that this Army to which they had committed and covenanted their lives and service maintain and continue what founders William and Catherine Booth set out as the way ministry should be, the Raders observed the lack of equal ministry between men and women in the United States of the 1980s. They yearned to see and advocated strongly that their Army return to those early guidelines, to utilize all the gifts and talents available among its officers regardless of gender.

Of course, not everyone within the Army welcomed this bold move by the Raders. Paul's brother, Damon, remembers that "attitude toward this was a mixed bag. Some are affirmed and liberated . . . some feel threatened, uncomfortable."

Whatever the reaction, however, Paul and Kay Rader were discovering God's guidelines for their priorities and their leadership for the years to come. Several sturdy pillars supported their ministry. One was a global vision, a worldwide view of the kingdom of God beyond one's immediate locale. Another was equality of ministry opportunity for the Lord's called ones with no respect for gender. And ever since college days, Paul Rader believed in cooperation between The Salvation Army and other Evangelical branches of Christ's Church. Above all, the Raders committed themselves to giving their best to the Master, whether it be honing the mind, disciplining the body, or reaching out with sensitivity and compassion to human beings whom God wants to gather into His family.

And God did not neglect Paul and Kay, two members of His family still feeling the loss of their Korean home and all it meant to them—raising children, launching ministry, surviving hardship, developing kinship with a strong and sturdy people. He honored their obedience with blessing.

The Rader phone rang one summer day in 1984, and Paul found their friend Henry Holley on the line. Holley was longtime director of overseas crusades for famed evangelist Billy Graham and now had an invitation for Kay and Paul.

"Come with us to Seoul for the centennial celebration," he said.

In 1884 the first Protestant missionaries landed in Korea, and in 1984 a significant series of events to recognize that turning point in church history was underway. Holley served as the Billy Graham Evangelistic Association director for the centennial celebration.

"I worked with Dr. Han Kyung-jik and the Centennial Committee for the preparation of the meeting," Holley said. "In the process, it was my recommendation to Billy Graham that we invite Paul and Kay Rader to come to Seoul for this meeting. . . . These dear, wonderful people had made such a contribution to the spiritual life and growth of Korea." Dr. Graham, recognizing the Raders' contribution to Christianity's spread across the peninsula, agreed with Henry Holley and invited them to travel back to Korea to share the joy.

Holley had observed the Raders during his frequent visits to Korea for the Billy Graham Evangelistic Association and calls them "two of God's finest servants . . . no, 'slaves,' for Jesus Christ. A servant can come and go and is employed with certain rights, whereas a slave has no rights and has been bought with a price to do as the master directs. So, Paul and Kay were perfect examples as slaves of Jesus Christ."

For Kay and Paul this invitation meant another glimpse of the land they loved; to use their hard-won language skills; to shake hands and hear news from former cadets and coworkers; to see, smell, feel, and rejoice; to experience closure and easement of the grief over separation from Korea and its people.

God tends His family with tenderness and compassion. This the Raders knew as they returned to their United States appointments after the centennial celebration, eased and energized by a remarkable reunion with the people and places that would always feel like home and family to them.

11

1986-1989

IN THE SALVATION ARMY the path toward leadership usually follows a fairly predictable route. As in baseball, Army officers headed toward significant responsibility must touch bases one, two, and three before arriving triumphant at home plate.

The Army in the United States is a formidable operation. In 2000 its four territories encompassed 1,327 corps community centers nationwide; 61 outposts, which are places of worship and ministry not yet organized into full-fledged corps; 3,845 service units; 87,502 senior soldiers (adult church members), 15,753 adherents (those who attend but have not yet joined); and 37,219 junior soldiers (*Salvation Army statistics,* end of 1998). It invaded North America for God in 1880, and through the following 120-plus years its path to top leadership developed in a predictable manner.

Paul and Kay Rader, however, were finding themselves propelled along a course that departed frequently from the norm.

"We're rather weird ducks—we've always been so from the beginning." Thus Paul describes their service in The Salvation Army and their steps toward leadership.

"When we came back [from Korea to the United States] we were a totally unknown quantity in terms of leadership capacity," he says.

Kay adds, "I think some tended to discredit the experience we had in Korea. To them it simply didn't count."

Paul served as training principal in Korea, teaching and administering the school in the brain-bending Korean language. Following those years, he was appointed Education Secretary for the territory.

"Next thing I'm Assistant Chief Secretary and then, a year

later, Chief Secretary," Paul says. "And Kay was appointed Acting Territorial President [of Korea's Women's Organizations]."
This required more stretch for their language skills as everything
from legal documents and headquarters directives to personal
counseling and polite chitchat—in Korean—had to be added to
their teaching and public speaking opportunities.

"Normally the Territorial Commander's wife serves as President," Kay says, "because of the ill health of two successive Territorial Commanders' wives, I was twice appointed Acting President."

Even so, the Raders came back to a United States appointment
as unknowns when it came to leadership or administration. This
bothered them a bit, this fact that their experience in Korea did
not seem to count in the thinking of their American comrades.

Commissioner Andrew S. Miller, long a friend and mentor to
Kay and Paul, wanted to do something about this and lent his influence as United States National Commander to the Rader appointment back in the United States. His goal? Not to elbow God
aside and maneuver the Raders—two people he had prayed over,
watched, and advised throughout their careers—toward stellar
posts or places, but to lend his influence to build in them the specific experience that would generate respect and the understanding within The Salvation Army that here were two people the
Holy Spirit had used and would continue to use. Miller wanted to
do all he could to insure that Paul and Kay suffered no lack of
tools or resources for whatever God had in mind for them.

Apparently the American Commissioner said as much to General Burrows when planning the Rader appointments, because the
General, herself a missionary at heart, had other international
posts in mind for Kay and Paul. Miller's advice was "Put them on
a track of exposure to a variety of experiences in preparation for
leadership. They need to gain the respect of the people."

He believed that they must develop a feel for the workings of
The Salvation Army on a wider scope, to learn divisional responsibility. Miller knew about the opening coming up in the eastern
Pennsylvania/Delaware (PenDel) division. He talked with Commissioner Stanley Ditmer, who was responsible for the Eastern

Territory, expressing his sense of the leading of the Holy Spirit, that gentle nudge he had learned to heed, and Ditmer agreed that the Raders should have the job.

So after three years of training officers for the Eastern Territory, Paul and Kay received a new appointment in the same area where Paul's Grandfather Damon was Commander 50 years earlier. It broke in on them on a Friday night. Paul had just come from a huddle with those in charge at territorial headquarters in New York.

"You'd better sit down while I tell you this," he said to his wife. Kay sat. "We're going to the PenDel division."

Appointed by Commissioner Stanley Ditmer, eastern Territorial Commander, and approved by General Eva Burrows in London, Paul called this move into divisional leadership "huge." Kay, too, knew a serious challenge lay ahead of them. Neither of them had ever worked on a divisional staff, an appointment far different from the cadet training they had done in Korea for more than a decade and now in the United States as well. Having skipped service on divisional staff, considered almost a requirement on the way to senior leadership, contributed to their "weird duck" status—certainly in their own thinking if no one else's.

Paul says of this appointment, "My knees got watery when they told me, because I thought, *I hope you guys know what you're doing.* They were taking a big chance on us."

Some of the factors that weakened Paul's knees were a huge divisional budget for which he would be responsible; boards to chair; oversight of Camp Ladore, one of the Army's largest, which lay within his jurisdiction; pastoral responsibility for officers and 45 corps; and a multitude of social projects and institutions.

It was as if Paul Rader's miniature army of toy soldiers once deployed across the kitchen table of his childhood had suddenly grown to life size and were fighting hard for God in the PenDel Division. And Paul was in charge.

But in retrospect, Juanita Russell claims that Paul and Kay "had the gift of pastoral leadership. They'd go anywhere an officer was in trouble—and they had a lot to deal with. . . . The division is 'down in the trenches.' They could handle it."

Major Juanita Cochran Russell, along with husband Reginald, were on the PenDel Division staff, he as Divisional Secretary and she as League of Mercy Secretary. Reg, himself an Army child, knew the five Rader kids well, and Juanita, a Georgia Methodist pastor's daughter, had encountered Kay countless times at Indian Springs Camp Meeting. Both were Asbury College graduates.

As a member of the divisional headquarters team in Philadelphia, Juanita saw the Raders do battle in those trenches. Given their unflagging dedication to mission, one of her observations of the Rader partners comes as no surprise. "They awakened the division to the world," Juanita says. "They created awareness of what was going on. They got people concerned."

Coupled with mission came partnership, of course. Of this Juanita makes her observations from her American point of view. "Partnership is not as big a deal in the U.S. as in some parts of the world. It's not so unusual here," she believes. "I never felt suppressed. My husband encouraged me to speak whenever possible so it was not an issue for me."

But at the same time she says, "Kay was a forerunner to bring issues to the table, which was not necessarily understood by some people."

Juanita feels that perhaps the fast-track appointments that characterized the Raders' movement through Army ranks at this time might have stirred jealousy in some, plus Kay's being an outsider, not raised in a Salvationist family, as Juanita was not, could have created skepticism and opposition to her trailblazing ways. "Some people just hate change," she sums it up.

"The Raders stood in the forefront of women's issues," Juanita acknowledges. "Because of their intelligence, they set in motion that from which others will reap benefits." She cites how they modeled teamwork in public ministry alongside their jogging and fitness. "Intelligent, forward looking, visionary, they were really spiritual leaders" is her summation of Kay and Paul.

Watery knees or no, Lieutenant Colonel Paul Rader arrived at divisional headquarters in Philadelphia with certain carefully prayed-over goals in mind. First was to learn, an excellent antidote for skimpy knowledge and experience. Paul also brought to their new appointment a burning desire to see corps grow. In "An Agenda for Our Future," his message at their welcome celebration, his guidelines for growth included a "burning sense of mission and evangelism" that's "grounded in scripture." The new Commander wanted to pursue the "cultivation and activation of officers," focusing especially on women in ministry, developing the full range of their capabilities.

Rader complimented the PenDel Division on the range and quality of its social ministries. In surveying Army patterns, he observed, "We tend to respond somewhat cautiously—in some ways our strength . . . and we will exercise prudence." But he also wanted to see the division's impressive array of social services operate on the cutting edge. "We want to be responsive and timely in our response to the urgent needs confronting us."

Paul was especially concerned about teenage pregnancy, for, having already read up on his new post, he knew that Philadelphia had the highest teenage birthrate in the nation. He cited a litany of human miseries confronting The Salvation Army at the time: teen suicide, prostitution, substance abuse, abortion, illiteracy, homelessness.

The antidote? That the Army's front-line warriors "embrace the world for which Christ died," and that those warriors focus on the Word of God and renew their emphasis on prayer.

In tandem with these purposes, Kay came to Philadelphia more sensitized than ever to women's issues. She made the enabling of women called by God to ministry in The Salvation Army her top priority. When asked about attitudes toward this emphasis among their coworkers, both Raders replied in unison, "Some liked it; some didn't."

Commissioner Miller, in reflecting on the Raders' efforts to sensitize the Army to the business of married women's call to ministry, says, "Kay read Army history. She knew that our beloved Catherine Booth envisioned a leadership union . . . they took some criticism [and] did it with dignity."

Learning was job-one on Paul's list of goals, and he plunged into an intensive tutorial on handling United States Salvation Army employees, a platoon of volunteers, and a high-powered advisory board, not to mention dealing with regular crises and public issues. He also pastored his flock of officers across the reaches of the division, and as a recognized master of the art, he taught preaching.

"Philadelphia taught us an awful lot, particularly in the area of social services," says Kay, "the nitty-gritty of what it's like to be poor in America, to be hopeless."

Although they cut their missionary teeth on dealing with the poverty and deprivation of post-war Korea, Paul and Kay had not confronted it at length in America. "This opened our eyes to things in our own country that we had been away from for 25 years. We needed Philadelphia."

The officer from the inner-city corps next door to divisional headquarters knew he was welcome to drop by the Commander's office and talk, which he often did. To illustrate for his Commander what he contended with, one morning in a moment Rader can never forget, the officer reached across Paul's desk, opened his hand, and dropped a bundle of used syringes. "I picked these up by the kids' play yard this morning," he said.

Such pain and disappointment did not bypass the Raders. Even as a recognized church growth guru and coming off dramatic successes in Korea, although some lagging corps experienced reactivation, Paul Rader saw no new corps planted in his division on his watch. This was mainly because of financial limitations that made risk-taking impossible. A competent and conservative Financial Secretary committed himself to protect his Commander from budgetary over-extension, which he knew would certainly create problems in the eyes of his superiors at territorial headquarters, so funds never seemed to stretch far enough to include the risks of new church plants.

In his mentoring work toward developing and strengthening officers, especially among people of color so crucial for leadership in the city's ethnic mix, Paul had to grapple with the disappointment of seeing some of his brightest and best leave their ministry for various reasons. Add to that the times when the ones departing blamed their Divisional Commander for not coming to help in their moment of crisis, and the pain level had to be high.

Especially when he and Kay drove for hours to be there, and the officers chose to allege otherwise. Or when a former beneficiary in the Army's prison prerelease program who appeared ready for employment picked up an ax while on the job and attacked several people within his reach, killing three.

Some lessons one would rather do without.

Kay and Paul put plenty of miles on the Divisional Commander's car as they trekked between corps and projects, speaking opportunities and people in need. A pattern of reading aloud to each other that began back in Louisville while Paul studied at Southern Baptist Theological Seminary became fixed into habit as they traveled. Early on, Amy Carmichael books rode the miles with them, and ever since, reading to each other is as consistently on their personal agenda as their daily run; they read everything from biographies and best-seller fiction to French philosophers and theological tomes.

But then it was again time to pack their books and everything else. Just into their second year of learning and innovating within the PenDel division, the Raders found themselves nudged into a wider place. From Philadelphia to New York is not so far geographically, but the responsibility quotient in the Army only grows heavier as one accepts an appointment higher on the ladder.

Paul and Kay's move to New York included a promotion to Colonel, Paul's assignment to the territory's Chief Secretary job—higher visibility and more responsibility. Paul says about it, "Commissioner Ditmer went out on a limb to take us."

Kay plunged into her responsibilities as Home League Secretary for the territory with Commissioner Catherine Ditmer as her respected mentor.

An interesting indication of how God maintains balance and perspective for His obedient ones is the attitude of the Rader team toward each move. They felt no impulse toward ladder climbing. By their own assertion, they could have stayed contentedly in the training school in Suffern when the appointment came to the divisional command in Philadelphia. Of the school, Kay says, "We loved it there. We were not looking for greener pastures."

Even as they were executing the move to New York City, people around them suggested they shouldn't unpack. A leading officer said to Paul, "You see what's happening, don't you? You won't be there long."

Paul replied firmly and frankly. "No, I make no assumptions about what's happening." Even though some seemed informed about the Rader future, they were not eager to hear about it.

"We realized that something was going on," Paul says. "In fact, the Chief of the Staff wrote to say we would not be there long," something he and Kay shared with no one. Commissioner Cox wrote from London a letter full of implications about the future. "My dear Colonel, I write to confirm my cable sent today." From that cable the Raders had learned they were to say farewell to the "present appointment," for Paul was appointed Chief Secretary for the United States Eastern Territory "with rank Colonel." There was no mention here of Kay's rank or appointment.

Cox did say, however, along with his congratulations and good wishes, "In this I naturally include Mrs. Lieutenant-Colonel Rader and pray that God will grant to you both grace and wisdom for the responsibilities ahead."

The letter's final paragraph was a touch out of the ordinary, for the Chief wrote, "The General desires me to say that this appointment will be for a number of months, a further change being envisioned later in 1989. It is hoped that you will not find this too unsettling but that you will both give to Commissioner and Mrs. Ditmer that loyalty and devotion to the cause of Christ that has been one of the precious hallmarks of your service through the years."

Ignoring the hints and whispers that swirled around their promotions and new appointments (even though Commissioner Cox said that word of the brevity of this appointment was "for your information only"), Paul and Kay unpacked every box, hung every picture, re-covered the couch, and invited family to visit their new quarters on the upper west side of Manhattan as they plunged into their assignments at territorial headquarters. They were keenly aware that only God knows how long any appointment will last. Even though they were told not to unpack completely, that their tenure would be short, they settled in.

Paul loved his "busy desk," he called it, and enjoyed to the full the Chief Secretary's responsibility as second in command in the territory. Included in his duties was participation in the Commissioners' conference—comprised of all Territorial Commanders and Chief Secretaries—which sets policy for the nation.

He just plain enjoyed making things happen and there was plenty of that for him to do. He may have found many similarities between the Eastern Territory and the Korea Territory where he had also served as Chief Secretary, but at least in the U.S. he could do it all in English without the encumbrances of translating, speaking two languages, and zigzagging between cultures.

The time in New York was God's gift to Paul in a personal way. His mother, Gladys, lay near death in brother Herb's home on Long Island, and living so close by enabled Paul and Kay to visit her often. The first time he stepped into her room after his appointment as Chief Secretary, Paul had to grin as she turned toward him and called out in her quavery voice, "Hail to the chief!" No one told her, sick and deaf as she was, of her son's appointment. The family was mystified. Where did she get her information?

And when Lieutenant Colonel Gladys Damon Rader finally received her promotion to glory, Paul and Kay, along with their Rader brothers and sisters, stood singing around her bed, honoring the valiant and godly woman who took a strong hand in shaping each of them—none more so than her son Paul—into useful, contributing members of God's Army.

For the service celebrating her promotion to glory, Lyell Rader Jr., her youngest child, wrote a tribute to their remarkable mother. Citing her "talent for loving," Lyell spoke of how she brought to her marriage "the saving qualities of sensitivity, humor, decorum, and grace."

As the evangelical sword of her husband was unsheathed across what he termed ever-widening "war paths," she found her gift and task, especially during the child-rearing years, pre-eminently in the home. Here her quiet regal spirit was pervasive and led her children to cherish with her the beautiful, the genuine and the true. She imparted unconsciously her sense of duty, of order, of *noblesse oblige.* She was a patient listener, a gentle encourager, and to her final hours, a tireless intercessor.

Her husband and children, grandchildren and great grandchildren bear witness to the benediction of her love.

1. Paul and Kay with children at Army day care center, Sipovo, Bosnia, 1996.
2. Kay with Rwandan children orphaned by genocide, 1994.
3. Paul signing autograph for children in New Zealand.
4. Kay meeting Bangladeshi recipients of micro enterprise grants, who are now self-sufficient.

1. Cartoonist's impression of Paul "holding forth."
2. Paul and Kay with Lt. Colonel Royston Bartlett, aide-de-camp, in Belfast, Northern Ireland.
3. Commissioner Kay preaching the Word.
4. Paul at South Pacific East Asia Zonal Conference, Seoul, 1999.

1. Kay at Salvation Army maternity clinic, Colombo, Sri Lanka.
2. Paul with resident of Notintone House, Nottingham, England.
3. Paul with farm family assisted by the Army in Sipovo, Serbska, Bosnia.
4. Kay with young Brazilian at Army center, Vila dos Pescadores, Brazil. Children signed T-shirts for the Raders.

1. Paul and Kay at AIDS center in Mumbai (Bombay), India, with, *from left,* Captain Sureesh Pawar and Commissioner T. G. Sundaram (in white uniforms). "Here, healing is happening on the inside," commented one member of the group.

2. The Raders with delegates to the International Youth Forum, Cape Town, South Africa, 1997.

3. Kay being interviewed in Palu, Indonesia.

4. With aide-de-camp Lt. Colonel Royston Bartlett at Blind School, Kingston, Jamaica.

5. "If two shall agree"—Paul and Kay at conferring of honorary doctorates, Greenville College, Greenville, Illinois.

12

1989-1994

CALIFORNIANS WHO LIVE in the San Francisco Bay area will not soon forget the 7.1 earthquakes that hit during rush hour October 17, 1989. Neither will Kay and Paul Rader, who had stepped off a plane from New York a few short days earlier to assume new appointments in The Salvation Army's Western Territory. The territory's biweekly publication, *New Frontier*, announced that the Raders would take over as Territorial Commander and President of Women's Organizations October 1, following the retirement of the Commissioner and Mrs. Willard Evans and the Raders' own promotion to Commissioner. After the brief eight months that Paul served as Chief Secretary at Eastern Territorial Headquarters, the move predicted for the Raders less than a year before by the Chief of the Staff materialized.

So, properly on deck for a smooth handover, Paul and Kay were moving through the fetes and fact-finding that accompany Army torch-passing when death and destruction hit California's fabled city by the bay and its environs.

The night before the catastrophe, the Southern California Division had celebrated the 40th anniversary of the famed Los Angeles Billy Graham Evangelistic Crusade, which had propelled Graham into international attention and swung open doors of opportunity that across decades led countless people worldwide to accept Jesus Christ as Savior and Lord. He received the William Booth Award that evening "for outstanding contributions to the betterment of humanity through four decades of international ministry" (*New Frontier*, November 4, 1989).

As soon as he heard about the earthquake, Paul prayed over and weighed what his personal response should be. Of course, the Army in the area was out en masse with food, clothing, water, shelter, and counseling both for victims and those who came to aid them. Should he stay out of the way and let them continue uninterrupted doing what they do so well? Or should he go and make visible his concern and support? His ego didn't demand the exposure, but neither did he shrink from what leadership requires. As he prayed and pondered, a phone call from his National Commander and old friend Andy Miller assisted in Paul's decision.

"Have you been up there yet?" Miller asked.

"No."

"Go! You'll never regret it if you do. If you don't, those people will never forget it."

Paul booked a seat on the next plane for San Francisco, intent on talking with people affected by the disaster and seeking their opinions as to how the Army could help further. He calls Miller's advice good "because I tended to feel that they've got people in charge—they can handle it. Which they could, but the important lesson I learned was that the leader must show his or her face."

Adding to the mix, Billy Graham, who had stayed in California after the Army's anniversary celebration to work in seclusion on his autobiography, called to say, "If you invite me, I would go up." He wanted to see for himself not so much the damage as the people. Graham and Paul Rader toured the disaster sites together, and "by the end of the day he [Billy Graham] had talked personally with hundreds, praying with them and, in their names, left The Salvation Army $100,000 from the Billy Graham Evangelistic Association" (Judy Vaughn, "Evangelist Tours Army Earthquake Relief Sites," *New Frontier,* November 4, 1989).

At the time of their appointment to lead the Western Territory, Kay and Paul were promoted to Commissioner, a rank that "engages high respect," according to General Arnold Brown's autobiography, *The Gate and the Light* (108). He writes that the Army bears legal obligation to "keep in office a Chief of the Staff [second in command to the General] and no fewer than twenty-one other commissioners." Given the fact that upwards of 25,000 officers supply varied forms of leadership in the Army, such rank "bespeaks selectivity and implies consequence. To this must be added the dignity, competence, achievement, and high

degree of spirituality which, through the years, officers have con-
ferred upon the rank, rather than the reverse." Consequence indeed. A serious weight of history and expectation accompanied
the Raders' promotion.

Hard on the heels of Paul's foray into the destruction zone
with Billy Graham came family from the eastern and southern
United States to help celebrate their installation as territorial
leaders in the west. *New Frontier,* in a front-page article by
Robert Doctor for the November 4, 1989, issue, describes a high
moment in the "ceremony of affirmation and promise." Andy
Miller conducted the installation and after his remarks "noted the
presence of Mrs. Commissioner [Kay] Rader's father in the audience—a retired Methodist minister, and also recognized the presence of Rader's father, Lt. Colonel Lyell Rader, O. F. (Order of
the Founder)." As Kay and Paul knelt at the Holiness Table, their
fathers joined them, one on either side, as did Miller and his wife
"for a season of prayer and sealed the installation in a sensitive
and quiet moment of personal commitment."

Within a few short weeks came a watershed moment for the
Western Territory of The Salvation Army and for the Raders'
lives and commitments made before God during their installation
as leaders in the West. They embarked on an endeavor that would
define their tenure there.

Seeds of change had sprouted at an international congress
held in London in 1988 that centered on Army growth. General
Eva Burrows called for "holy daring." She stated that the Army is
called to facilitate "change in our communities without losing
our unique character." "Let's grow!" was her central theme, and
the movers, thinkers, and shakers of the Western Territory heard
her message loud and clear. After the congress Paul Rader called
in Peter Chang, Bill Hunter, and Terry Casey for a brainstorming
session, people he knew would be able to come up with fresh, innovative, Spirit-prompted thinking about how the Army could
grow in their region. The initial session developed into regular
times of dreaming and talking and praying over the most effective ways to discover and work toward what God had in mind.

MISSION 2000, they called it. It would be a full-bore effort to double the size of the Army in the territory—the number of corps, of attendees at those corps, and of cadets in training, for obviously they would need more leaders for the multiplying corps. It was as simple as that, but bordering on overwhelming in its audacity.

The better part of a year passed as Paul's brainstorming group, variously referred to as a think tank or a round table, dreamed their dreams and did their homework. Terry Camsey, Evangelism Secretary for the territory, remembers that the round table group took no minutes. Paul encouraged them, he says, "to think outside the box." These dreamers became the architects of MISSION 2000, for their Commissioner changed "maintain" to "grow," which is what they intended to do.

When they brought to the table the doubling idea, Paul says, "I had some misgivings about the boldness of the goal to double," but as they studied what had happened in the Christian and Missionary Alliance Easter campaign, in which that denomination actually doubled the number of its churches in a decade, it seemed possible. After all, the Raders' predecessor, Commissioner Willard Evans, had said to them, "The West is a sleeping giant." This they believed, aware that they had walked into a ripe situation.

Therefore, blazing *New Frontier* headlines launched the effort, announcing MISSION 2000 and its plan to double the territory. Their mission statement: MISSION 2000 is a bold, faith-based venture to double the number of corps and corps officer/ leaders, and to secure at least double the number of soldiers and Sunday attendance by the year 2000. Paul Rader shared the fire that burned within him with passionate words that *New Frontier* published in March 1991.

"Is it time to hear again the Pentecostal call, to see visions and dream dreams as never before?" He harked back to Peter's sermon to new believers "on that fiery first day of Pentecost," when Peter quoted the prophet Joel: "Even on my servants, both men and women, I will pour out my spirit . . . . I will show wonders in the heavens and on the earth, blood and fire and billows of smoke. . . . And everyone who calls on the name of the LORD will be saved" (Joel 2:29-30, 32).

Rader pointed out that demographers promised "explosive increases for the western states," but in spite of the Army's significant growth, "we are not beginning to keep pace with the population." In short, "we must move, accept the challenge of MISSION 2000." Joe Noland, then General Secretary in the Los Angeles division, says that at that time the Army was maintaining the status quo. "Growth from a church growth and evangelical perspective was not taking place."

Then Chief Secretary for the territory Ronald Irwin admits to being a "foot-dragger for a while . . . but then I could see what he was doing. My fears were groundless."

In the Raders' travel across their vast territory, Paul often challenged officers and laypeople alike to look ahead and think about growth. In March 1991 he defined it for the Alaska Congress Officers' Meeting: "Growth . . . has to do with the reproduction and nurturing of life. It is not about bricks and mortar—not first. It is about people coming alive in Jesus Christ . . . about the growth of the Body of Christ . . . about the sacrificial commitment of living persons in order to accomplish the purpose of our living Lord . . . the advance of the Army . . . and the salvation of the world!" (Rader sermon notes)

For the remaining years of their appointment to the Western Territory and their relentless emphasis on growth in that territory, the building blocks that Paul and Kay Rader lifted into place alongside their team of fellow dreamers and doers were hewn from the same foundation stones that characterized their ministry from their earliest junior officer days in Korea.

EVANGELISM AND CHURCH GROWTH

In *Red Hot and Righteous: the Urban Religion of The Salvation Army,* Diane Winston claims that a shift in emphasis occurred in the Army after World War I toward social services and away from its storied evangelistic efforts (see chapter 5). In the epilogue, however, she wrote, "Whether staging musicals based on the life of Evangeline Booth or performing rap concerts in lower Manhattan, Salvationists continue to use the vernacular culture in evangelical crusades—even if their image as street-savvy soul savers has been eclipsed by their reputation as dependable providers of social services" (250).

Evangelism is basic in the lives of both Raders. Kay watched evangelism introduce her mother to a personal relationship with Jesus and saw how her father evangelized his workers and their neighbors by building the little church in which they worshiped. Evangelism was lifeblood to Lyell Rader, and a young Paul easily saw the importance of telling people about God's redemptive love. To draw others toward the Savior was the primary goal of everything they did from college days, on through their Korea years, and in each appointment thereafter.

Paul told his Alaska officers, "We will serve people. We must. . . . And they come by way of the Mercy Seat. And what MISSION 2000 is about is placing 200 more Mercy Seats in communities across the West and surrounding them with caring, praying, serving people with a heart for God and for the lost. Out from there will march the Army of the future" (sermon notes).

LEARNING

The fact that Paul Rader loves books and learning goes without saying. The fact that his doctor had to tell him to put down his books and exercise his body if he wanted to live speaks to the single-minded devotion he brings to mental discovery. Kay equals him in this and adds her special dimension of wanting to learn about people along with studying ideas and issues. At their welcome in October 1989, Kay spoke of her joy at being in such a beautiful place, asserting that people make places beautiful. "We're listening for the sounds of the West, your heartbeat," she declared (*New Frontier*, October 18, 1989). And in January 1990 Paul directed a specially appointed commission to discover the effectiveness of the Army's response after the Bay area earthquake. They reported back to him and other administrators so they could learn from the disaster.

Even though some of their coworkers and friends describe Kay as the more approachable of the Rader partners, they also say Paul is a good listener, that he seeks input. "Paul listened and affirmed" in meetings, Doris Noland says, "before disagreeing. He articulated the issues well, never putting anybody down."

Paul and his think tank listened carefully as the consultants they chose talked about the verities of The Salvation Army in their region. They learned that the Army was strong in reputation as well as resources, that North American Baby Boomers needed their message and that growth was possible.

LEADERSHIP DEVELOPMENT

Officer recruitment was crucial to the doubling goals of MIS-SION 2000, and quite naturally those involved looked toward the officer training program and applauded when the number of applicants grew. Bill Hunter, part of the original crew, says that thanks to innovative recruitment methods, their number of cadets climbed to the highest on record since the 1920s.

Paul, however, conducted some leader cultivation on his own. A year after their arrival in the West he appointed Joe and Doris Noland as divisional Commander and Director of Women's Organizations in Hawaii, and Paul, according to Joe, "took some risk in this." Noland claims that they were "out of favor, free spirits, innovative in approach," and they "challenged the status quo of conservative administration."

"Along came the Raders," Joe remembers, "who were very empowering, releasing, in their leadership style. . . . We'd always felt we were swimming against the flow. All of a sudden, when the Raders came we were swimming with the tide. It felt so good . . . I can't even tell you how good!"

During their three years in Hawaii, Paul gave the Nolands freedom to try new things. They consequently opened new corps in the island state and expanded Salvation Army work in Micronesia, all with their Commander's support. He then appointed Joe to the cabinet in the west as Program Secretary and handed Doris responsibility for current issues, followed closely by League of Mercy duties.

In the acknowledgments of his book *No Limits,* Joe Noland wrote of the visionary leadership of Paul and Kay Rader, saying that it "challenged, inspired, released, and empowered. They took us to places we had never been. They saw the invisible and did the impossible."

Dan Starrett ran The Salvation Army's Adult Rehabilitation Center (ARC) in Seattle when Paul approached him about expanding his responsibility to taking over the whole territory, which meant 3,400 employees, $120 million in thrift store sales, and a multi-million-dollar combined budget, not to mention the thousands of men and women who come to the Army for help with their addiction problems, who need care, counsel, and tough, loving communication about God's solution for their difficulties.

"Commissioner, I'm flattered," Dan said when Paul told him what he had in mind. "I sure hope you know what you're doing." Dan pointed out that he was a mere 42 years old and that the ARC program was vast and complex.

"Why is it any different for you than for the president of the United States?" Rader queried. "He's 42."

Won over by the faith in him evidenced by the commissioner, Dan said, "Sir, I'll do my best."

Paul Rader, according to Starrett, has an "uncanny ability to be aware of circumstances but doesn't allow them to soil him. It's a special anointing of the Holy Spirit." He is challenged by Paul's ability to "not allow anything to restrict his thoughts and growth." And when Dan suggested to Rader that since the ARC people find it difficult to integrate into regular corps even after they're clean and converted, they should think about establishing ARC corps. Paul agreed. Soon there were four, going on five, of them, and it's working well. Women assumed leadership of some of the centers, and cadets, eager to be trained for Salvation Army service, are coming out of those corps.

"Rader challenges you to think beyond where you are. Whenever I'm around him, I'm challenged to that," is how Starrett sums it up. Paul says he finds great pleasure in "trying to mobilize people to realize more of their potential for growth and innovation."

WOMEN'S ISSUES

Kay's concern about the utilization of women called by God into ministry is not something she grapples with alone. Years before their appointment to leadership in the Western Territory, she and Paul—by talk and study, observation and experience—

forged unity between themselves on the issue. They committed to doing everything in their power before God, not only in sharing equally their own ministry opportunities, but also by lending their growing influence to aiding women within The Salvation Army to flourish, to find freedom from prejudice or neglect, as they obey God's call to ministry.

Ron Irwin, Chief Secretary of the Western Territory during the Rader years there, remembers that Paul was the first Territorial Commander to include wives—women with comparable rank and the same call to ministry as their husbands—in the cabinet meetings, not only to include but also to encourage to participate.

A telling section in Ronald Thomlinson's biography of General Frederick Coutts, *A Very Private General,* illustrates a more common attitude about the disposition of female leaders. Coutts, it appears, in recognition of his writing and editing skills in 1935, was appointed to the editorial and literary department at international headquarters in London. Coutts had his work, it says on page 52, "but there was a large element of frustration for Mrs. Coutts. Possessing a trained mind, having been a teacher, and ten years the wife of a busy corps officer, now she had no other responsibility apart from her family. . . . Mrs. Coutts had now the difficult task of discovering a completely new life-style for herself." This kind of waste is anathema to Paul and Kay and is contrary to traditional Army practice as set forth by the founding Booths.

The MISSION 2000 campaign developed a strong emphasis on women's contribution to its goals. A shift in focus away from centerpieces and gift-wrapping and toward more substantive issues and opportunities for women soldiers and adherents promptly followed seminars and training sessions tailored especially for Army officers. In May 1991, in keeping with the Raders' emphasis on women, in a *New Frontier* editorial Commissioner Kay Rader took on J. I. Packer, who opposed women's ordination and public ministry in churches in a piece he wrote for *Christianity Today.*

Her boldness in confronting this Evangelical icon stimulated some letters of appreciation from those who read her article, but even so, not everyone agreed with nor appreciated the Rader emphasis on women in ministry. Ron Irwin admits he did not—at first. Initially reserved in his support for MISSION 2000 in general, he acknowledged that Kay also annoyed him then. It seems her "aggressive methods" troubled him more than her agenda.

Esther Sather, who leads the League of Mercy in the Western Territory, remembers Kay's keynote address when the Raders took up their appointments in the West. Kay spoke on current issues, Sather says, and made it clear that "she didn't do bows." The women directors at territorial headquarters were "micromanaging, and she told them to stop it," to focus on matters of importance. The women "enjoyed Kay's pushing them to be more. . . . She always pushed them into professionalism," and they involved themselves in addressing the issues of pornography, euthanasia, and so on, and in getting information out to their people.

Philip and Keitha Needham, Western Territorial Secretary and Women's Organizations Secretary, worked with the Raders during their tenure in London and acknowledged that "Kay was often misunderstood, was considered pushy." Some even think she violates biblical teaching, but "Kay was willing to pay the price" of misunderstanding and negative comments.

It is interesting that in the mid-19th century when Britain's Commissioner George Scott Railton assembled his initial Army assault team to sail to the United States in 1880, he selected "sturdy, stable women," the leader of whom, Captain Emma Westbrook, "had never heard of wearing a uniform and had no certain notion where America even was, let alone why she should go there." In the first of several farewells, "the speaker prayed for God to 'drown 'em' on the way if they were going to fail Him when they got there!" (Edward H. McKinley, *Marching to Glory,* 13). One way to deal with pushy women!

The Salvation Army legacy as told in literature and history reveals a divided heart when it comes to its women officers, trained and commissioned equally with the men, and at times handed what the Christian world considers "a man's job" but at other times ordered to stand back and stir the soup, preferably quietly.

But the world contains an Army of women warriors called by God to service, and they are not about to disappear by drowning or discrimination.

INTERNATIONALISM

Two factors made it impossible for MISSION 2000 to be a growth incentive merely for white, Anglo-Saxon, Protestant Americans. One is the reality of the ethnic rainbow in the United States, especially in the Army's Western Territory. The other emanates from the Raders' hearts and souls. Everyone who knows them, even briefly, comments about their worldview.

"They wanted officers and civilians to become world Christians"—Gordon Bingham.

"He [Paul] elevated cross-cultural work. . . . Now the fastest and most exciting work [in the Western Territory] is ethnic"—Philip Needham.

"Paul promoted ethnic diversity, asking, 'How come no Hispanics, no blacks?' [on committees]"—Robert L. Doctor.

"The Raders can fit into any culture—it shows"—Janette Bosanko.

"He [Paul] is a world citizen by heart and action . . . sensitive to the chronic ills and new threats in the global village. Millions are still doomed to misfortune and oppression, and he hears their cries for salvation"—Check Yee.

Writers peppered the pages of *New Frontier* with accounts of kids on summer mission trips, research teams who go to the world's trouble spots to learn and to show that The Salvation Army cares. The paper chronicles the opening of corps for Koreans, Laotians, and Vietnamese, plus mission corps in the Marshall Islands and Alaska, and in June 1991 Bill Hunter wrote about the candidates needed to lead the expanded Army as a result of MISSION 2000.

"We know that the people we need represent a cultural and ethnic rainbow that includes Anglos, Hispanics, Blacks, Koreans, Chinese, Laotians, and Marshallese" (*New Frontier,* June 16, 1991, 5). Hunter said later in reflection that "cross-cultural plants came easier. They always seemed to have leadership potential, the Latinos and the Koreans."

And in the September 30 issue, Terry Camsey wrote of the first meeting of the MISSION 2000 Council, at which Paul Rader "affirmed that each of the 32 members was there specifically to share his or her expertise and input as it related to MISSION 2000 goals." Among the group of officers, commanders, and specialists of several kinds also emerged another breed. "Reflecting the ever-changing population mix, a representation of cross-cultural experts also participated." Even when striving to expand Army influence in the western United States, those who worked, plotted, and prayed could not ignore God's waiting world.

Kay tells of her kaleidoscope of impressions in Seattle, where they went to dedicate a new Laotian corps. "Uniforms, welcome gifts, leis, an indigenous worship service—I was home! So wonderful, so cross-cultural. We were in heaven."

Explaining her joy and delight in serving the Western Territory, she says, "Such things happened to us many times. Every cross-cultural experience like that produced ecstasy! It couldn't have been better."

The international outreach of the territory, even as they worked to expand at home, sent the Raders on several journeys to other parts of the world. To Russia, Chile, and Sweden at the direction of General Eva Burrows, and then when Major Check Yee asked Paul, his Territorial Commander, to join the Army team headed to China's southwest Yunan Province to dedicate a new high school, of course he agreed. The San Francisco Chinatown Corps, led by Yee, in empathy had responded to a severe earthquake in western China by raising $330,000 among Asian-Americans in the Bay area via a three-hour telethon, funds which went to rebuild and furnish the demolished school.

Yee reminisces about their journey, parts of it spent bumping over rutted, washed-out roads in the hinterlands. Of Paul he says, "He gets up at dawn, earlier than most people . . . greets each new day with a steady jog outdoors in the fresh air. . . . He sees the crowd in the streets, in the shops, getting ready for the day's toil. Who knows what burdens will come upon them, or what joy will cheer them up?"

Yee first met Paul in 1969 in Korea, where he was "attracted to his integrity and a spirit of compassion which compelled him to leave his home in the United States to spend more than two decades in a mission field."

Yee, well known in the San Francisco area, was the one who "appealed to television viewers to reach out with their checkbooks to donate funds" for relief of the families of the dead and displaced among the mountains near China's border with Myanmar (Burma). The results of his appeal enabled "distribution of blankets and food to thousands . . . and the completion of a beautiful, three-story high school to replace the one destroyed by the quake."

Yee admits that traveling in Yunan Province, China, is not pleasant, and "due to the exotic new diet and changes in climate, Paul was the first one to be sick. He sat in the small van seat, his long legs cramped in the piles of luggage."

"Commissioner, you can't get sick. You are our leader."

"No, *you* are the leader," Paul said to Yee.

Yee claims, "I was always proud to present my Territorial Commander wherever we went. He was always prepared to give an appropriate message on the spot—brief but powerful, based on gospel truth."

Before a thousand people at the dedication of the new high school named Mercy, Paul said, "The name 'Mercy' is a gospel word which will not be forgotten. For what we have done is not engraved in stone alone, but inscribed in the hearts of the people, 'a letter from Christ . . . written . . . on tablets of human hearts'" (2 Cor. 3:3, RSV).

Not all went smoothly on the trip. As the van left Gangma, the town where the new high school was built, "suddenly a torrent poured on the mountains, flooding the roads up to our knees," Yee said. The van "floated in deep water. The bridge ahead broke . . . the darkest night of horror."

Police came to the rescue. Toward dawn Yee and Rader found themselves roommates in a damp, chilly, small room with wet mattresses in a cigarette factory. In one corner was the constant rhythm of leaking from the roof.

They read the Bible together from Psalms, Paul's favorite book according to Yee—Psalm 46:2-3 in which the writer asserts that he will not fear "though the earth give way [which it had that day in western China] and the mountains fall into the heart of the sea."

That night Check Yee spoke to Paul of something he had wanted to say for a long time. He watched Paul read his Bible by candlelight and then said, "Commissioner, I have a deep conviction that one day you'll be the General of The Salvation Army. And I pray that you will."

"Thank you," Paul said with surprise in his eyes.

"One of the reasons I wanted you to visit China is that when you become the General, you will remember what you have seen here. Should any proposal for China come to your office, you may give supportive consideration, instead of knowing China as only a dot on the map."

"Well, one-fourth of the world's humanity is a big dot," Paul responded.

Check Yee was neither first nor last to make such a prediction to Paul Rader. Insulated, however, by the power of the Holy Spirit through the habit of ceaseless prayer, Paul seemed to ignore such remarks, never savoring, never repeating to others the dreams held for him by some of his friends and coworkers.

PRAYER

Upon the inauguration of MISSION 2000 in 1991, Terry Camsey announced in the March 1, 1991, *New Frontier* headlines, "Territory Seeks 200 Prayer Intercessors." He called for 200 "Power Partners who will pray daily, particularly for those starting *new* corps or outposts." A quote appears in bold type beside Camsey's article: "'Now is the time to bathe this whole vital process in prayer'—Rader."

In the Easter 1992 issue of *New Frontier,* in which potential new corps sites are revealed and Commissioner Rader writes about the risen Christ opening the doors to Mission 2000, on page 2 Robert Doctor reveals that the appeal for Power Partners surpassed its goal by doubling it.

"The Lord knew best," Robert Doctor wrote, "and provided over 400 intercessors: more than twice the number asked for and, surely, symbolic of the Lord's blessing and confirmation of our goal to double the Army presence in the territory over the next decade."

Kay and Paul depend on prayer in every facet of their lives.

When a toddler, Kay's life was spared thanks to Mariah's prayers. Paul sat with his sister and brothers around the table as his father, a formidable prayer warrior, rattled heaven's gates on their behalf. Prayer stabilized them through times of abundance and abasement in Korea; it saw their children mature into discerning, God-fearing adults. Kay taught prayer to literally thousands across the years and the miles, from Korea to Pennsylvania and points in between. And God provided powerful prayer partners for MISSION 2000, people who promised to surround the new corps and the new leaders of those corps as they sprang up across the territory.

So, of course, the Raders prayed as the date for General Eva Burrows' retirement drew near. Her retirement meant that the High Council would convene at Sunbury Court outside London, where Commissioners and Colonels with senior command appointments would gather and, following prescribed procedure, would elect someone from their number to succeed her. In General Arnold Brown's 1984 autobiography, *The Gate and the Light,* Paul marked a passage. "All agree, however, that the procedures of the High Council in selecting an international leader for the Army are more a spiritual exercise than the employment of ordinary electoral processes. The incomparable fellowship, heightened by much prayer and reading of the Scriptures, has all the features of a highly devotional spiritual retreat. Imperceptibly, the appraisals of possible nominees are shaped and, as voting draws near, a sense of guidance, flowing from the Holy Spirit's presence, possesses the delegates' minds and hearts."

Paul boarded a plane for London in April 1993 to join his fellow officers in choosing the next General at the Army's 12th High Council. Fifty gathered in all—36 commissioners and 14 colonels. Three women stood among the bevy of men, all three of whom held territorial commands in Indonesia, Sri Lanka, and Zambia/Malawi.

Paul Rader's name appeared among eight others at the balloting for nominations. Among the eight, two declined immediately. Each of the remaining six, as is High Council custom, spoke at length about his dreams for the future of the Army and offered prepared responses to probing questions from the councilors, prepared and approved in advance regarding current issues with which The Salvation Army grappled in its worldwide outreach.

First balloting results saw three nominees withdraw. The second balloting eliminated another. Only Bramwell Tillsley and Paul Rader remained. The president adjourned the session for a half hour of prayer. "Following prayer and the third ballot, the president announced that the result was again inconclusive, being short of the required 34 votes for the two-thirds majority. Upon resuming with a period of devotions and prayer, the fourth ballot took place, which now required only a majority vote. The president then announced the outcome" (Henry Gariepy, *The History of the Salvation Army, Vol. 8, 1977-1994*, 289-90).

The 12th High Council had elected Commissioner Bramwell H. Tillsley [General Burrows' Chief of the Staff] as the 14th General," Gariepy continues, "to take command of The Salvation Army on 9 July 1993. Commissioner Rader expressed to the General-elect his own congratulations and pledge of loyalty."

Close call? Brush with destiny? Paul, of course, talked over the experience of promise, possibility, and the remarkably narrow margin of rejection with his partner, Kay, and with his Redeemer in his place of prayer. He then plunged back into his duties and opportunities in the Western Territory. No lack of challenge there. And as was the case in Korea, in the PenDel Division, at the training college, and at the Eastern Territory Headquarters, they flourished in the place God planted them and did not yearn for higher ground.

13

Thoroughfare for the World

ON MAY 5, 1994, Paul Rader preached arguably one of the most significant and affecting messages of his long and lustrous public speaking career. The Salvation Army in the United States had called a National Forum centered around the theme "Toward the Twenty-first Century," and Paul, according to *The War Cry* in the June 18, 1994, issue, "gave an impassioned keynote address titled 'Vision 2000—Where Are We Going?'"

Working up to the moment when he would speak in Chicago to the 1,380 delegates, Paul admits to worrying about the appropriateness of his message, an uncommon dilemma for him. But according to Captain Steven Bradley's *War Cry* report, Rader graphically and effectively pointed out "the clearly downward spiral of today's pervasive 'value vacuous' culture." And because he seems always to be able to see over the barriers, no matter how high, he trumpeted, "The fact is, there was never a more exhilarating time to be a Salvationist," and insisted that the Army "must be fully open to explore new directions," an admonition which surely failed to surprise either his devotees or his detractors, for it was this advocacy of change and innovation that equally stimulated fellow change agents and troubled those dedicated to maintaining the status quo. The Raders had been aware for some time that leadership in North America was as resistant to change as any in the Army world.

Sure of his ground, Rader outlined for his listeners 12 "key areas for Salvation Army advance, each introduced by a bold 'forward!' Into new communities . . . toward greater diversity . . .

equalization of status . . . the inner city . . . response to human need . . . changing funding structures . . . greater ownership by lay Salvationists . . . not to mention innovation in ministry models and fresh approach to mission and to corps." Finally Paul urged his listeners to "lift up Jesus, high over all! Then we will be ready for the twenty-first century and beyond!" (Rader sermon notes).

Many of those who heard the Western Territory's Commander that day say he aroused in them a remarkable awareness that here was a man sent from God with fresh thinking and a passionate heart, a man who stirred their spirits within them, a godly man worth following, and a significant number of those who may have balked at Rader's innovative urgings found their resistance melting away under the power of the Holy Spirit. General Albert Orsborn told of his youthful observation of Army leadership early in the 20th century, and Paul Rader unwittingly fit his description: "Such people were not potters with the obvious. Their addresses were not mere refrigerated verbosity, coming out of cold storage! They were venturers, inspirers, revivers!" (*The House of My Pilgrimage,* 34).

A major shock fell in on the Army world just 15 days after Paul's ringing call to American Salvationists to avoid being "a closed community of the thoroughly initiated committed only to our own self-preservation, muttering to ourselves in a code language baffling to the average citizen and off-putting to the serious seeker." "I am concerned," he had told them, "that we not become a kind of secret society . . . more concerned about preserving our idiosyncrasies than being faithful to our essential calling—privatistic, self-absorbed, and effectively neutered! That Christ alone may have the first place in . . . our purposes, our priorities, our planning, and our programs" (Rader sermon notes).

Even as United States Salvationists, following Paul's ringing exhortations, sought to reevaluate their purposes and priorities, their General, Bramwell H. Tillsley, relinquished his post. Henry Gariepy tells how it happened in *Mobilized for God* (300).

"On 20 May 1994, the Army world was stunned by the announcement . . . that General Bramwell Tillsley had on 18 May

relinquished the office of General." Tillsley took this unprecedented step after a brief 10 months in office "for health reasons,
effective immediately. The immediate and unprecedented relin-
quishment of the Army's highest office sent a seismic shockwave
throughout the Army world, and confronted it with uncharted and
difficult waters to navigate. The Salvation Army for the first time
in its history was without a General." In June 1994 *The War Cry*
carried a short piece explaining that the 63-year-old Tillsley had
undergone a triple by-pass operation and that "the considerable
burdens and demands of the office have taken their toll on his
health. The General said that his decision to retire had been a difficult one, but it was undoubtedly in the interests of the movement and his own health."

Paul and Kay were at the American Commissioners' Conference that May day, preparing for an early-morning run before the
first session, when their phone rang, abruptly aborting their exercise plans by summoning them along with the other senior leadership in the United States to a special 7 A.M. meeting.

"We knew it was something dramatic, to meet at 7 A.M. When
we got there, Commissioner Hodder made the announcement
that General Tillsley had relinquished office for health reasons,"
Paul remembers. "That was a terrific shock! Before we got out of
the meeting room [after the announcement], one or two people
made the comment, 'Well, you're next.'"

But neither Rader was looking for promotion. The West was a
wonderful place to be, and going through the election process
again held no charm whatsoever. Paul turned aside their well-
meant comments by saying, "You're very kind, but that remains
to be seen, doesn't it?"

On May 26, however, the summons to the 13th High Council
arrived, and Paul Rader, along with 43 other commissioners and
colonels, had to return again to Sunbury Court outside London on
July 19 to participate in the election of a new General. Just days
before he left, Kay and Paul spent a day hidden away in a motel
room in California, a day of praying, reading, thinking, talking.

"We were not at all sure if Paul were nominated that we wanted
to accept," Kay says. "We had settled in to go on with MISSION

2000 there in the West. We had gone over shaky ground on a couple of issues, weathered them, and felt that God wanted us to stay—maybe even retire there. I perhaps more than Paul considered what it would do to our family." Kay knew it would entail a loss of privacy for their children and grandchildren, creating a vulnerability to public scrutiny they did not choose. And for both Kay and Paul, a nomination would require them to face the possibility of a second highly visible and much discussed rejection, a prospect most difficult to contemplate. Paul says his reluctance centered around questions concerning what the Lord wanted.

"If God didn't want you in 1993, why would He want you in 1994?" he said.

How did they resolve these questions? "We prayed on our knees all day," Kay says.

Paul knew that "it was important we both be on board, because it involves, as we found out, a lot of physical effort, vulnerability, exposure, and plenty else." They had to weigh these demands against the fact that they were well and happily situated where they were.

"I didn't know whether I wanted to go through that or not," she remembers. "I did not want to be just the General's wife. I had no aspirations for that."

So how does one deal with such a prospect? "We had to pray until we were willing to let the world march through our souls" is Kay's answer.

At the end of their day of prayer had they reached that point?

Paul: "Yes, we had."

Kay: "More or less."

Paul: "Oh, I think we had. We said we had. We went forward from there. I left soon after for the High Council."

Kay, of course, did not go to the High Council. "Mrs. Commissioners," in spite of their rank, were not included—only the husband half of commissioner couples. She went instead without Paul to a Rader family reunion at the Gabrielsens' home in Greenfield, Indiana. Sensing, perhaps, her deep concern, a delegation of nieces and nephews plus her own children gathered around her, put hands on her head, and prayed for her.

"I was in a real emotional state," she admits. "I don't think I was quite ready to consider that it might be. Maybe I said yes because I thought it wouldn't happen, because I had always believed they would never elect an American General."

The fact is that throughout its long and impressive history, Salvation Army Generals had been British, Canadian, Finnish, Swedish, or Australian. Never had anyone born in the United States been elected to the post. Evangeline Booth, first woman General and daughter of the founders, was a naturalized American citizen, an action she took before assuming leadership in North America.

On the morning of the election Kay went out for a run and "ended up under a tree, crying out for peace about this thing," she says. "God met me there and gave me peace."

When Kay returned to the house, brother-in-law Ted met her. "How are you doing?" he asked.

"I'm OK now. I think I'll be all right no matter what happens."

Later that day, July 23, as the whole family milled about in Jeanne's gracious kitchen, the phone rang. Paul was calling from Sunbury Court to say the High Council had made their decision, electing him the 15th General of The Salvation Army. When Kay told the family, hilarity and celebration broke loose at decibel levels for which Raders are famous.

Then on Sunday, Kay says, "We had this marvelous gathering before they all went home." Rader siblings and their children shared prayer requests, some quite personal. Kay's request was that God would protect her from becoming inured to and jaded by big congresses and meetings, for she knew she and Paul, as international leaders of The Salvation Army, would spend much of their time in such gatherings. She asked for prayer that she always receive a personal blessing no matter how many she went to. Also, she needed the Lord's help to endure "Mrs. General" jokes.

"They prayed for me there," Kay says.

And without question every Rader family member old enough to realize what was taking place half a world away in England prayed for Paul as well. In contrast to the noise and love

filling the Gabrielsen home, at Sunbury Court Paul stayed alone
in a small room just up the stairs. During the days of their delib-
erations, which broke records for brevity, he rose and ran each
morning, often pausing for a moment with God in a tiny green
park nearby.

Aware that Kay stood surrounded and supported by family
during these pivotal days, Paul focused on the events of the
Council. Each of the High Council attendees knew she or he participated in a historic first for The Salvation Army. Because Tillsley had relinquished office, the Army had no General. When the
votes were counted, the new leader would step immediately into
worldwide responsibility without benefit of transition or torch
passing. The insignia lay on the table before them and would be
attached to the shoulders of the one they chose.

Paul was chosen unanimously on the second ballot, a proce-
dural first, and he stood in the midst of The Salvation Army's
worldwide senior leadership as other hands took away his commissioner insignia and replaced them with gold-edged General's
epaulets.

Kneeling immediately, Paul asked for prayer, knowing not all,
but enough to be aware that he and Kay were entering into the
heaviest responsibility and most demanding years of their service
for God within The Salvation Army.

Long years before, a much younger Paul Rader did some un-
derlining in his copy of General Albert Orsborn's autobiography
titled *The House of My Pilgrimage*. In a chapter called "Election,"
Paul marked where Orsborn describes his feelings when the High
Council voted him into the generalship. "The General is not merely the titular head of an organization—he inherits a spiritual trust
which is not just a repository of ideals but is a tradition of vision,
inspiration, holy example, and dedication to God" (155).

On page 157, again underlined in red by Paul Rader, Orsborn
bares his feelings about the election. "I was not elated: this was
not a victory, since I had not done anything nor had I competed
with anyone, to attain this position. It struck me as a conferment,
a trust, not an attainment."

Then Orsborn wrote something that, had he had time to read

it while at Sunbury Court, would have resonated in the deep places of Paul's heart. "My first private thought, running strongly beneath all else, was of my mother. I wondered if she, in the world beyond, would know. . . . I thought of her, with great reverence and tenderness."

When the vote was completed, several High Councilors spoke to Paul about how pleased his father, Lyell Rader, who received his promotion to glory just a few months prior, would have been at this moment, the man whose youngest child and namesake— another Lyell—called a "Salvationist zealot." And even as he nodded in acknowledgment of their kind and thoughtful words, Paul's mind again turned to his mother, the valiant, dedicated woman who fought her war in the shadow of her famous husband, loving and guiding and shaping all her children, forming strong, abiding ties with her middle child who now stood at the head of the Army to which she committed her life and her gifts, who, with his wife Kay, must now keep that Army on the march.

In *My Utmost for His Highest,* Oswald Chambers wrote, "God breaks up the private life of His saints, and makes it a thoroughfare for the world on the one hand and for Himself on the other. No human being can stand that unless he is identified with Jesus Christ."

In the October 8, 1994, issue of *The War Cry* is an article titled "We Must Go Forward." Its heading says "In these excerpts from a speech to the High Council that would elect him General, Commissioner Paul A. Rader calls for 'an advancing Army amid the meanness and misery of the world.'"

In his speech Rader painted with bold and vivid strokes that meanness and misery and the Army's role in it. "But our field is the world and that world is aflame! Our sinning, suffering planet is exploding in crisis, while bursting with opportunity."

Because of that opportunity, he questioned the idea this was a time for "settling down comfortably, for bringing up the drawbridges . . . and hunkering down against the storm of an unfriendly world in our citadels of safe spirituality and Salvationist camaraderie, isolated and effectively neutralized. . . . What would the Founder say to us here? I think . . . one word: 'Forward!'"

He spoke of "special forces" to take on "innovative evangelistic strategies and services" that "might serve to raise the whole level of our commitment and help to break us out of a defensive and conservative mode, lest, in some places, we die of our own dignity!"

A sidebar on page 11 of that *War Cry* issue lists a couple of immediate decisions taken by General Paul Rader "in consultation with other leaders." One was the "appointment of an international relief team to establish several children's villages for 100,000 abandoned children affected by the Rwandan crisis."

Within months Rader also appointed six Territorial Commanders, two International Secretaries, three Chief Secretaries, and "an officer commanding." Not surprisingly, among them were "two single women appointed as Commissioners. At the time of the appointments, no single women had held the rank of Commissioner."

Paul and Kay Rader's concern for the world and for women called by God into ministry affected the newly elected General's decisions as soon as the distinctive insignia were fastened to his shoulders. God was breaking up their private life and making it a thoroughfare for the world, and that world had begun its march through their souls.

14

Never More Needed

FOLLOWING HIS ELECTION JULY 23, 1994, at Sunbury Court, General Paul Rader spent a couple of weeks in London at The Salvation Army's International Headquarters dealing with issues and decisions already stacked up and waiting on his newly acquired desk. Paul had met media representatives briefly and answered their impromptu questions outside Sunbury Court immediately after receiving the General's insignia and requesting prayer from his fellow leaders. For his first formal press conference held at International Headquarter July 26, however, he crafted an eloquent statement. In it he cited some of the world's worst problems and situations, asserting that he was "convinced that there never was a time when a *Salvation* Army—and that, an Army on the march into the future—was more needed in our world."

News releases emanating from International Headquarters and from the Community Relations Department of the Western Territory stimulated even the secular press to note the Rader election as evidenced in news columns carried in the *Washington Times,* the *Beacon Journal,* and others about The Salvation Army's first American-born General. Christian magazines like *Christianity Today* and *World* printed the news as well. Of course, the Army's various publications worldwide rushed into print with lengthy articles about their new General, complete with color layouts and numerous photos.

Army historian Henry Gariepy says that at the time of Paul Rader's election to the Generalship, "strong winds of change [were blowing] across the landscape of the international Salvation Army." He cites increasing urbanization and secularization, ideological realignments, and redefinition of the role of women as "all helping to shape a new sociological context in which The Salvation Army would carry on its work" (*Mobilized for God,* 309). Into such change came Paul and Kay Rader, frequent advocates of change themselves as international leaders of the Army.

Bill Hunter, one of Paul's roundtable cohorts on MISSION 2000, speaks of his "great sense of rightness" over the Rader election. "It was a time of Salvation Army transition out of the past," Hunter says, pointing out Army need for new vision, new methodology, and new understanding of theology. "Paul's education brought a trained mind, international experience with compassion and heart, and willingness to move across cultures. All this combined to make an ideal leader."

Commissioner David Edwards, an international himself and qualified to comment on the issue, had said, "If any American becomes international leader, one who has exposure to and understanding of the rest of the world, it's Paul Rader."

He explains: "Paul and Kay were people the Army needed to call attention to the changing world, where you have to do mission differently. They were not shackled to the past, not afraid of risks—the kind of leaders the Army needed."

Colonel John Bate, secretary and aide-de-camp to two other Generals, wrote in a short essay, "We DO Have a General," about the requirements laid on every General's shoulders and said that during his five years in the Western Territory as Commander, Paul "displayed every innate virtue required to cope with the challenges. . . . Added to this, he is the epitome of kindness," which motivates, encourages and instills confidence.

Commissioner James Osborne calls Paul Rader "one of the great communicators in the Army. . . . the best preaching leader we've had for a long time." Osborne speaks honestly of his "mixed emotions" over the election, for he feels the Raders are "splendid leaders" but personally does not feel "in tune with some of the changes," all of which he "can't embrace . . . but supports many of them" although he declined to specify which he supports and which he cannot.

Among the decisions Paul made even before returning to the United States to collect Kay, to say farewell to the Western Territory, and to prepare for the move to their London-based assignment, was to appoint Commissioner Earle Maxwell as Chief of the Staff, the sensitive second-in-command post Maxwell held in the Tillsley administration. Also, Rader chose Major Royston Bartlett as his aide-de-camp, the one who would work with and accompany him and Kay through every step of the miles, years, and tasks ahead.

Bartlett was born into an English Salvation Army family in Croydon, south of London, and at age 14 felt called by God into ministry within the Army. He had been General Tillsley's private secretary and was enthusiastically recommended to Paul by mutual friend and Korea missionary veteran Commissioner Fred Ruth. Even though they had never met before, when they did, Royston felt an "immediate spiritual bonding." "Our souls touched," he says.

Mrs. General Kay Rader, as the General's wife, became World President of the Salvation Army Women's Organizations and, in continuity with her goal at multiple previous appointments, committed herself to "try to help women realize their potential for ministry . . . to be someone to stand in the gap for them in any way I could." In a word, she wanted "to try to keep Catherine Booth's dream alive."

Doris Noland looks back over Kay's influence in the United States before she and Paul were elected to international leadership and acknowledges that "Kay helped raise awareness of the long drift away from Catherine Booth's ideas" on women's ministry. Husband Joe admits, "There's still chauvinism in the Army."

Bill Hunter, in talking about both Raders' communication skills, says that time has proven that Kay, too, is gifted, citing "the re-emergence of women's ministry" under her high-profile advocacy.

After memorable farewells in the Western Territory, the Raders were welcomed, installed, and dedicated by retired General Eva Burrows at the Westminster Central Hall on September 1. During the ceremony, witnessed by a multitude of family, Fullers and Raders alike, Paul commissioned the team he appointed immediately following his election to go to Rwanda in central Africa in response to disease, homelessness, and death in that war-torn land. The team's assignment? To initiate special children's villages where victims of the fighting—an "estimated 100,000 abandoned children and unaccompanied minors"— could find shelter and peace (Gariepy, 324).

In so doing, General Rader acted in concert with an Army specialty of long standing. As General Coutts pointed out in *No Discharge in This War,* "The Salvation Army is expert—has been so for over a century—in the social and spiritual ills of the world's regions where its people work.

"The Army's social services were not born out of any doctrinaire theory but out of the involvement of the Salvationist himself in situations of human needs" (102).

Then in late November Kay visited the team in Rwanda to encourage them and see their work. What she saw and learned and experienced during those days of moving among the destitute victims birthed in her an abiding love for Africa and its people. It also strengthened her admiration and appreciation for the officers who spend themselves in the hard places without fanfare or notoriety.

As the Raders assumed their duties at International Headquarters, on Queen Victoria Street in the shadow of St. Paul's Cathedral, of course they brought with them strong ideas of how some things should be done. In keeping with their mutual desire that Catherine Booth's dreams for women in ministry be kept alive, they modeled for the Army ways to do exactly that.

As had become custom, when creating the General's schedule at congresses and conferences around the world, no one expected that Kay would speak unless for a women's meeting or to give a brief testimony before the General took the podium. This was tradition, after all. But the Raders decided that Kay should speak in all meetings, that her ministry should be a regular feature of every event. "We had to revise programs sent to us, because it wasn't anticipated that this would be true," Paul remembers.

"The reason for this was to empower and affirm all the gifted women out there who rarely saw a married woman leader do these things. Seeing us in action, they might decide, 'Hey—it's OK for me to get up and do these things.' They needed to see that. We felt the point needed to be made, and it was not lost on them."

Wherever they went, the Raders received appreciation and affirmation from young officers for their innovative ways when it came to public ministry for married women officers, ways that stood in place over 100 years earlier when The Salvation Army was born.

Royston Bartlett, even as he performed his protocol duties and tried to make sure the Salvationists they ministered to around the world did not "work the General to death," felt the impact of the Rader partnership. Royston knew that Paul never went into any kind of ministry situation without considering Kay's part in it all as well. "It was a different way of looking at ministry than I had come across in the U.K.," he says.

Royston's painful, tragic divorce had come about because his wife, an officer, sought and was denied the chance to be a "full minister in The Salvation Army. Then the climate was that this was always the man's role. They wanted you to be married, but then they forgot the wife was a minister, and that is something the Raders changed. Forever."

Even though these innovations on behalf of women came too late to save his marriage, Royston felt no hardship in serving both Raders, although his appointment was secretary, and then later aide-de-camp "to the General." They were a team, "the three of us in it together," and this was because of the Rader partnership. Royston knew this was the only way to go forward in The Salvation Army regarding women's ministry.

Bartlett's devotion to his role as aide-de-camp enabled Kay and Paul to function at maximum capacity during the years of their leadership. Paul defined the aide's varied and demanding responsibilities in 1999 after their treks to 75 countries: "The aide-de-camp to the General is the direct personal assistant to the General. He arranges . . . schedule and travels with the international leaders around the world." He "gives oversight to secretarial and support staff."

"The position requires good judgment, absolute confidentiality, and the highest standard of spiritual integrity. It is intensely demanding, administratively, physically, and emotionally. The requirements of physical stamina, efficiency, personal loyalty, and dedication are daunting."

There's more, having to do with travel arrangements and responsibility for personal safety, health, comfort and well-being. Rader says the aide-de-camp works "in the background," providing assistance, which may include "being travel agent, buffer, shield, mine sweeper, advisor, listener, chaplain, and companion," with "humility, graciousness, a sense of occasion, discretion, an instinct for protocol, alertness, helpfulness, and a good sense of humor."

So with this impossible job description in mind from the beginning, God's troika—Rader, Rader, and Bartlett—set out on a relentless itinerary capable of felling a venerable English oak tree. When asked if he knew the reason for all the travel, for all their appearances in 75 countries, for countless hours in message preparation, in handshaking, in listening and loving, Paul cites Col. 2:2—"My purpose is that they may be encouraged in heart and united in love." They wanted, Paul says, to take a "sense of connectedness with the Army globally so Salvationists in India, in Russia, in France would know they are not alone, that they are "bonded in common purpose and mission." General Rader sought to instruct through his hundreds of addresses "what is essential and central to our message—who we are, what motivates us."

Kay articulated it in an interview for *Mission Quarterly,* an Army periodical published in the United Kingdom. She told her questioner that because their role was spiritual leadership, they needed "to keep the focus on the priority of mission . . . to empower people to fulfill their calling regardless of age, gender, or giftedness." She also believed they were to "listen and learn, then to interject and translate." Her final goal was to "keep the movement united and Salvationists focused and faithful to God."

Royston remembers "meetings, so many meetings, tired of meetings, and then suddenly you would get touched." God didn't abandon them, for even if it wasn't the sermon of the moment, it could be "the sight of an old retired officer singing" that brought the blessing and reminder of why they were there.

Officers' councils became a specialty of Kay and Paul's ministry around the world. They always made them special, according to Royston. He recalls that they wanted to communicate what was "involved in ministry." Paul confirms this by saying, "I had an agenda of what I planned to talk to them about. Kay did too. We were selling our message to them, casting the vision."

This agenda always included reminders of the power of prayer and urging that Army officers around the world join the global prayer network that both Kay and Paul longed to see in force. And without fail they held up by word and example before their troops the banner of camaraderie and common commitment to mission from south to north, east to west, urging them toward relevancy, to keep abreast of current trends.

Royston, ever listening and watching in the background, admits to tilting toward thinking that perhaps Kay was too strong in presenting her message of a woman's right to minister until he saw how she connected with her comrades, how women clamored to speak with her, revealing that she was on target after all. In listening to her they discovered, "Perhaps there *is* a place for me in ministry." He insists that Kay's advocacy for women was never for their rights, but for the privilege of ministry.

Included in the agenda Paul carried wherever they went was the Million Marching Campaign he proposed at their welcome celebration in London, "a call for a major commitment to the recruitment of senior soldiers around the world" (Gariepy, 327).

"Everywhere we went, we would bang away at that," he says. As to where the idea came from, Paul seems as surprised by it as anyone. He had glanced at Army statistics and observed that around 800,000 senior soldiers stood on the roles and, ever the growth advocate, he challenged his hearers in Westminster Hall that together they aim for "a million marching into the new millennium, wholly committed to Christ and the colors!" (327). This certainly worked for Salvationists in Pakistan, according to Territorial Commander Commissioner Shaw Clifton, who says, "The Million Marching Campaign gave Pakistan an impetus that resulted in 28 percent growth in three years, a net gain of 10,000"—this in a nation not naturally friendly toward Christianity.

His responsibilities shaped Royston's view of officers' councils, for he was always on guard over passports, tickets, briefcases, schedules. He remembers the councils in all their variety. "Large ones in U.S. hotels, under palm trees in India, high in the Bolivian mountains, others alongside the River Congo in a little hall. We could hear the river running by." And at that particular council all three—Royston, Kay, Paul—remember the joy and excitement that burst from the crowd when they learned that each of them was to receive a mosquito net to take home, a life-saving provision where mosquito-born malaria rages in all its forms. A warming footnote to their joy was the fact that the corps in London that Royston's daughter, Lydia, attends provided the nets for their fellow Salvationists in Africa.

A milepost event in the Rader generalship was an International Youth Forum, a first for The Salvation Army, convened in Capetown, South Africa. Paul calls it "a seminal meeting in its impact on us and the signal it sent to young people around the world about the future of the Army." Among the events of that forum was a time when the young people from across the world, 500 of them between the ages of 18 and 30, brought their recommendations for The Salvation Army to its General and World President of Women's Organizations. The Raders spent hours over a two-day span publicly responding to each recommendation.

The General's challenge to the forum's 500 youthful delegates was simple, hard-hitting, and impossible to ignore. "I want you to reach out and take the nail-scarred hand of Jesus and walk boldly into the future He has for you. Beyond that door lies the true potential for you to become the Breakthrough Generation."

Their time and prayers given on behalf of this youth event seemed well spent when, Kay says, they learned that "many went home to their territories and commands and organized youth forums there with their territorial leaders." The time spent in Capetown was not just an inspirational moment or two. It provided serious interaction with tough issues; an opportunity for young men and women to share their dreams for the Army as well as their concerns. Debate was often intense and lively. Many made life-changing commitments as delegates grasped the limitless potential of their Army under the blessing of God.

Paul and Kay, as The Salvation Army's world leaders, also focused their energies on Latin America, researching the critical issues that affect Army efforts in that region, seeking to gain awareness of the thrust of the dreams and aspirations of the Salvationists who proclaimed God's good news in Latin America and the Caribbean. A Latin American Strategy Commission, which took shape under the direction of Commissioner David Edwards, gave voice to those dreams, put into action the aspirations for social concerns and evangelism alike.

The weeks and months raced on inexorably, filled with airplanes large and small, cars, and a remarkable collection of conveyances, including elephants and open carts designed to show off the General and his wife to the public, according to how guests are honored in each culture.

"It was just as important, more so perhaps, to the people," Kay says, "that we see them than they see us. The majority of their preparation centered on what they planned to do for us. Dances, songs, bands, marches . . . all for the General to see."

Royston remembers that in India the people "needed to touch the General." With dismay he watched as "hordes ran to touch, to feel," for his assignment was to protect and enable the international leaders of The Salvation Army. What could he do when Paul and Kay stood in a crush of hundreds of shouting, jostling enthusiasts? Paul acknowledges that the love of people around the world for the office of General is "a huge responsibility."

Faithful to his appointment, Royston Bartlett found that he had to screen people out at times, reminding them that the General was not their personal possession. For this difficult phase of his duties he endured considerable abuse, he admits, from those annoyed by his protective interference. Despite this occasional rub, Bartlett affirms that the Raders and their aide-de-camp *always* left every gathering last, "turning out the lights and putting out the cat," they called it. When asked if he approved of this behavior, Royston says, "Oh yes. It was vital. Necessary." According to him, "they never lost their natural touch. All those years in Korea, sleeping on the floor and all, made them real people."

How did Paul react to all the "General" adulation? "We didn't inhale a lot," he says, and acknowledges that he owes much to Royston and to Kay in helping him to avoid taking it all too seriously. "You need to recognize that it relates to the *role* in which you've been cast. You like to feel you bring something to it, and you certainly take it seriously and do the best you can, but ultimately the accolades and most of what is said and done relate to what faithful Salvationists have been doing out there for years and years. You know that."

Paul also knew that when the General is invited to see presidents and national leaders, it is because of the people on deck who do "a good job for Jesus. This has to be kept in perspective." They learned, for example, how the "people on deck" had laid groundwork for their gracious reception by the Crown Prince and Princess of Japan, whom they met at the Imperial Palace in central Tokyo.

The protocol officer gave them careful instruction about the logistics of their visit with the royals and their deportment during it. "You will converse for a half hour, and then when the door at the far end of the hall opens, you will rise and take your leave."

"But when we got in there," Paul remembers, "in there" being in a grand, glittering hall large enough to accommodate two basketball courts laid end to end, "they were just warm, friendly, and, of course, well educated, for they had studied in the U.K. and the U.S."

The Raders discovered that the royal family of Japan is well aware of The Salvation Army. The night before their visit with the Crown Prince, an uncle had attended the International Staff Band concert celebrating the 100th anniversary of Army presence in Japan. The Prince and Princess related that they had heard about the concert from him. That uncle had watched Army band marches in Oxford Circle, London, years before, perhaps as a student. Consequently, the Prince was more than cordial and keenly interested in Army activities.

The Raders stayed beyond their half hour, for the door at the far end of the room never opened. Had their highnesses waved off their attendants? Kay and Paul never found out, but their eyes widened when the Prince finally stood and said, "Now we'll escort you to the door."

The four of them walked the full length of the grand hall to the mammoth ornate doors, where the Prince and Princess saw them out in a remarkable gesture of Oriental hospitality from persons so highly placed.

Paul, with permission, had prayed with them at the end of their conversation, as he did with most other heads of state and high officials on their journeys. "I can't remember ever being refused," he says. "In China one time the fellow wouldn't close his eyes, but I prayed with him anyway. He let me do it." And in Georgia, once part of the Soviet Union, President Shevardnadze smiled broadly, the only time during their visit, Kay recalls, when Paul asked, "Shall we have a word of prayer?"

Sometimes strong and welcome affirmation of the Army came unsolicited from a head of state, as was the case of France's President Chirac, who told the Raders that whenever he struggled with a particular social problem, "I always call The Salvation Army."

Bartlett could never relax from his duties and thus does not call travel with the Raders "pleasure." "I was there to make sure they were safe" is how he sums it up, "except, together alone we relaxed and we laughed—laughed and cried all round the world. People often said, 'There's a special relationship between you and the Raders, isn't there?'" He guesses that because he had to be on guard at all times, perhaps the pleasure came afterward. *"Joy* is a better word," he opines.

Kay and Paul liked Royston Bartlett from the first, especially his great sense of humor, which was good for the rigors of constant travel. Looking back, they realize they never had a clash. Bartlett could even confront the General when, perhaps, stress tightened his nerves and made him a touch forbidding. "Oh, we have the General back, do we?" Thus he nudged Paul away from his role and its duties and back into relaxed good spirits once more. Or when Paul spoke of a decision he expected to make,

Royston at times made so bold as to say, "General, I think that's unfair."

"We were chaplains to one another" is how Kay describes their team of three. "We had no one else. We could build each other up in the Lord."

Small wonder that as he shepherded his charges from place to place, Royston Bartlett gave his all to guarantee their safety. In some countries he saw police on duty outside their hotel rooms. In others he listened and prayed as he heard kidnappings described, especially of Americans. At times armed guards rode in the front seat of their car. And there was the danger of being stampeded by their own jubilant people, who on a few occasions rushed up and rocked the car in which the three of them rode.

And what does a Salvationist aide-de-camp do at such moments? "Shout and scream 'Make way for the General!' . . . and it usually worked."

Royston's worst fear, however, was of losing passports and tickets for which he was responsible, a fear never realized. Close on the heels of that specter loomed the awful possibility of missing a plane, which never happened either, doubtless a tribute to his relentless dedication to duty and detail.

Kay and Paul found it all worthwhile—the preparation, lost sleep, ceaseless availability to others—when they found themselves in the company of those they call "the people who validate the uniform."

"Traveling around the world, how often Kay and I felt unworthy to wear the uniform when we saw these who wear it through sacrifice and persecution," Paul says.

"Before some of these officers you want to take off your shoes" is how Royston feels. "When you stand in their presence or hear them testify, you feel, well, 'I'm not worthy to wear the Salvation Army uniform.'"

Who are these people? In Brazil they met Captain Margaret England, whom they found living among the desperately poor, their rickety shacks hanging out over stagnant tidewater. She was sharing her love and obvious joy with everyone within reach.

In Zimbabwe they met Captain (Dr.) Dawn Howse, M.D., a

Canadian officer who without a thought for her own comfort does everything in the Army hospital from surgery to leading a brass band for kids after teaching them to play. "Just leave me here, General, until I retire," was her plea.

"We saw many Mother Teresas around the world," Kay says.

Certain moments they experienced will live in their minds forever: driving to the Army medical center on the Indonesian island of Sulawesi and being greeted by its Muslim citizens waving a welcome to the General with Salvation Army flags; standing on a scarlet-painted floor decorated thus to honor royal Russian martyrs of the revolution but now reverberating to the sound of new believers singing "Nothing but the blood of Jesus."

Royston Bartlett sums it up: "We traveled twice a month or more, and after the hassle of preparation (his specially tailored cross to bear) we always came home feeling the privilege of this ministry." As the three of them watched sinners seek salvation and believers submit to God's best for their lives, they often murmured together, "It's because we said yes all those years ago."

15

Partners in Mission

THERE'S NO QUESTION that God broke up the private life of the Rader partners. Serving as a thoroughfare for the world, as Oswald Chambers wrote, made personal, private time a luxury for these two very private people. Relating well to others and enjoying the interchange, they find their sustenance and strength in solitude. They shrink from the curious who seek to know and broadcast information about their personal lives and activities, an automatic treatment of those in such high-profile appointments. Kay illustrated this graphically in Anand, India, when she allowed herself to be photographed in her international gray uniform, smiling ruefully, beside a plaque quoting Mahatma Mohandas Ghandi.

"My life has been so public that there's hardly anything about it that people don't know."

Even when at home in London, Kay and Paul seldom let down their attendance to duty. After perhaps a 24-hour hiatus, a "brain-dead day" as Kay called it, during which they confronted jet lag, laundry, personal mail, and phone calls, they kept meticulous office hours, usually dealing with issues that piled up on their desks while they were gone. Never did the General or the World President content themselves solely, however, with reacting to matters that came up from across their worldwide Army bases; their hearts and minds spilled over with fresh ideas and opportunities for innovation they wanted to introduce in an effort to see their Army go forward at all points, just as they urged every time they stood to preach.

So while just down the hall from their offices Royston Bartlett worked with tickets, requests, and schedules involved in their next foray abroad, Paul met with Commissioner Earle Maxwell, with whom he had daily sessions when in London and on whom he depended to keep Army machinery running free of rust and breakdowns. Maxwell, Paul knew, wrote even the most difficult administrative letters with grace and almost always could make people appreciate even his reprimands. A fine public speaker and much in demand, Earle Maxwell took whatever task arose and handled it with dispatch and excellence. "He got the job done" is how Paul describes it, which was crucial to the ongoing implementation of Army policy over which its General presides.

Along with meshing with the Chief of the Staff when at headquarters, Paul also scanned the quarterly reports from all zones that brought him up to date on the progress, the conversions and discipling efforts of the Million Marching campaign, which he had defined in the Hong Kong Affirmation and then presented at London's Westminster Central Hall in November 1995.

"This is a statement of priorities in mission that God has laid upon my heart as we move toward the 21st century," he said. It reflected "the spirit and direction that emerged as a consensus" among Army leaders at the International Leadership Conference held in Hong Kong. One of those priorities, the growth of the Army by 20 percent—by this he meant spiritually mature soldiers "fully committed to Christ and to the colors"—would require "innovative evangelism, strategic corps planting, outreach to ethnic minorities, discipling of the young, conservation of our soldiery, and conscientious preparation of recruits for the serious undertakings of soldiership."

General Rader, still lighting fires as 40 years earlier he told his brother Damon he must, explained his commitment to this campaign for growth in the September 1995 issue of *The Officer* by pointing out, "We are, perhaps, the world's most widely dispersed, deeply experienced, and effectively organized Christian-humanitarian agency. Our hurting world needs the Army—in strength!"

Looking back later, Paul says, "We had to keep emphasizing that this was not about numbers but about battle-ready status, about readiness to do what God wants us to in the world as we look toward the new millennium. We don't want them on the books, but on the march!"

Both Raders knew that Army ministry to the "hurting world" was enhanced by enlarging to capacity the utilization of women officers, especially married women, who too often sat in the background instead of being encouraged to pull in double harness with their husbands or assume responsibility on their own. This knowledge influenced their executive action when in their offices or during their ministry in the 75 countries they visited, and is probably what prompted Paul's response to his first press conference question after his election as General.

"What is your overarching theme going to be?"

"Partnership in mission."

Reflecting back on his unpremeditated, whipcrack answer, Paul says, "That just came out of . . . somewhere. I feel the Lord gave it to me, because that's what we were about and what we wanted to do in terms of drawing our people together around the world, getting more commitment to global evangelization, while feeling ourselves a part of God's strategy. . ."

Kay continues, ". . . and establishing Army identity as part of the Evangelical church, partnering with the Evangelical world."

Even though the women-in-ministry issue arguably gained the highest profile during their tenure as Army world leaders, they meant, as members of the Body of Christ, partnership in all its facets.

"We made that the theme of our first International Leaders Conference in Hong Kong," Paul says of the gathering from which issued the Hong Kong Affirmation and also defined the Million Marching Campaign, "a conscious choice to have it (the conference) in Hong Kong with that particular theme rather than in England. We had never had one in the developing part of the world, never in Asia." Time had come to develop a sense of partnership with colleagues and other Christians regardless of national or ethnic origin.

What made the women-in-ministry issue so prominent in the whole business of partnership is Paul and Kay's conviction that the wasting of a significant portion of the Army's trained and capable fighting force cripples the accomplishment of all other goals. If women officers are encouraged and enabled to work as capably and as widely as the men, as is implied in their commissioning, will not the Million Marching goal be realized more readily? Are not new corps just as likely to be planted by women officers as men? Do not Christian women have documented gifts and graces for taking initiative in social welfare ministry? In preaching? In listening? Loving? In confronting sin and evil in all their forms? Are they not known to be willing and able to spend themselves for the sake of others?

The issue had been working its way to the Army forefront for some time. Henry Gariepy writes that during the 1994 High Council session, the one that elected Paul Rader as General, those gathered considered "key issues likely to face its elected leader." Among those issues was "the place of women in the Army, notably married women officers" (303).

Army coworkers and colleagues express themselves freely on the Raders' efforts to keep Catherine Booth's dream alive as it pertains to women officers. Commissioner Polly Irwin, affiliated with Kay and Paul on both United States coasts and a member of the General's advisory council, believes that their "working in tandem was a strength. They were role models for other officers." She notes, however, that Kay was "not one-sided. She is a good hostess, a people person." And as the crux of the matter, Polly says both Kay and Paul "made every part of their lives a matter of prayer, which brought extra depth and quality to their leadership."

Commissioner Berit Odegaard, a Norwegian officer who with her husband spent most of her service time in Africa, says she felt "excitement when they [the Raders] came in . . . a turning point! She [Kay] was unafraid. They worked together in ministry, an example, a breath of fresh air! . . . and the women in East Africa received their own rank."

What Commissioner Odegaard meant was a decision from General Paul Rader, who through his Chief of the Staff Earle Maxwell by letter notified The Salvation Army worldwide that "Mrs." was no longer a required part of married officer women's rank designation. No more would they be known as Mrs. Lieutenant, Mrs. Major. Now the speaking and writing of their rank would reflect the separate-and-equal commission they received at the end of their training when they stood side by side with their husbands as newly minted lieutenants. On that day "Mrs." did not define a married woman officer's status and would no longer do so in the days to come.

This decision did not come from General Paul Rader alone; it stemmed from recommendations from the Women in Ministry Commission established by General Eva Burrows several years previous. Chairperson of the commission, Commissioner Rosemarie Fullarton, Territorial President of Women's Organizations in Switzerland and Austria, reviewed the commission's report with General Rader in London, a report that would "generate major changes to elevate women officers to a more truly equal recognition and ministry" (Gariepy, 318).

Among the 10 recommendations presented by the 15-member commission, comprised of Asian, American, and European members, were "recognition of all officers by rank, Christian name, and surname, regardless of marital status . . . equality of consideration to be given to the vocation of all officers . . . every woman officer to be seen as a resource and developed to her full potential." In down-to-earth areas of a woman's life within The Salvation Army came suggestions for "a new system for calculating allowances replacing the tenure of married men officers as the basis," and "single women officers to have appointments of opportunity according to their gifts and abilities."

Paul acted upon their suggestions, for he wholeheartedly agreed. So, apparently, did at least one male African officer, for, flouting custom, culture, and public opinion, he stood before 7,000 of his peers to express his thanks for the decision that gave women—and he doubtless was thinking first of African women—rank in their own right.

The new steps in nomenclature, which seemed "just cosmetic" for some within Army ranks, cleared up confusion for a Kenyan officer, however, for he admitted that heretofore many in Kenyan soldiery had thought regarding women comrades "that 'Mrs.' was her first name. But now women have a name!"

Sensitive to the plight of women Salvationists, which was sometimes created by culture or perhaps by organizational fiat, Kay defined her role as "giving a voice to the voiceless." Indeed, when Kay was asked to plant a tree at a corps groundbreaking in the Ghana Territory, to her surprise she found that the women of the corps had placed a sign beside the tree. It read, "This tree planted by Kay F. Rader, Commissioner of Hope." Berit Odegaard's husband, Don, reflects on Kay's advocacy by claiming she "has done more for married Salvation Army women than anyone . . . not through feminism, but by producing excitement. She role modeled . . . she stepped on toes unafraid . . . irritated some people, but the days of wasting women are gone." He sums up his enthusiasm for the Rader partnership by saying, "There's new dignity now in The Salvation Army among married women."

And the changes continue. On May 1, 2001, word came from International Headquarters that Salvation Army rank would be revised, most notably that "service-year ranks," those received because of years of service, "in the case of married officers . . . will be held individually." This avoids penalizing officers who marry mid-career and have seen disparate lengths of service. For more than a century, women who marry men of lower rank lost their own in order to conform in status to their spouses.

The Army also gained dignity from a most unlikely quarter, for General Rader inherited a major problem in the form of an international investment fraud, which prior to his election had caused major funds to disappear from Salvation Army resources in the United Kingdom, money earmarked for aid to numbers of the nation's neediest citizens. Thanks to the diligence of a battalion of lawyers and investigators working with International Headquarters personnel, plus the prayers of scores of Army leaders, in less than three years the money was found and recovered—not only the total sum embezzled, but also legal costs and the interest lost in the interim. Paul presided over the restoration of these resources, mindful as he made statements to the media and stood in the glare of Britain's national attention, that dozens of others deserved credit for the miracle. And "miracle" best characterizes the resolution of the problem. Henry Gariepy writes in *The History of the Salvation Army,* "As a confirmation of the trust in The Salvation Army by the public in the UK, giving and support for the Army did not diminish, but actually increased in the wake of this crisis" (279).

Woven through their days in London in between overseas trips—days of meetings, appointments, encounters—both Paul and Kay had to chisel out blocks of time to prepare their messages for the next council, congress, or conference. Few knew what this cost them in hours, in research, in staying abreast of the times, in seeking the Lord's direction for what to say to the next spiritually thirsty crowd to whom they were to go.

Royston Bartlett had an inkling. Acquaintances occasionally sidled up to him after a meeting to ask regarding the General's message, "How many times have you heard that sermon?" expecting perhaps from him a sigh or some other acknowledgement of repetition and familiarity.

"Well, I hadn't," he sputters. He truly hadn't heard the sermon at all before then. "The same with Kay Rader. Very, very seldom did I even hear them repeat an illustration."

"And that came about," he continues, "because every night they would be in their own offices preparing. Never once did they get something out of their book that had been used before. Remarkable!"

Bartlett points out that while they often used the same text, the message was always different, for they never felt that what they prepared for the Russian people, for example, was what the Australians needed to hear. The same went for the Swiss and Indonesians.

From 1994 to 1999 Paul and Kay Rader trekked across the Salvation Army world, seldom seeing sights but never turning their eyes nor their hearts away from the people who came out to gaze at them and to hear what word from God they brought with them. They knew their assignment and refused to shrink from its demands. Did they make an imprint on The Salvation Army? Royston Bartlett, aide-de-camp and friend, offers arguably the most seasoned and intimate point of view on that question: "The British military has a saying—'a General is not a hero to his aide-de-camp'—but I can say Paul Rader is my hero."

Why such adulation from the man who read the mail, who scheduled the travel, who sought lost glasses, who waited for interminable conversations to end, who knew about wrinkled uniforms and 4 A.M. wake-up calls, who rode with the Raders in small sputtering planes and watched pilots try to determine where in the world the landing strip had gotten to?

For starters, Royston knew that the Raders were "not ambitious for the role. They were never pretentious, never used it for selfish aims. They always remembered it was given to them by God for a trust."

From the onset of Paul's time as General, they gave backing and assurance to leaders to try things, according to Bartlett. "The U.S.A. Western Territory was reborn whilst they were leaders there . . . and that went all round the world." He says that at the Hong Kong International Leaders Conference "You can!" became the watchword, urging Army leadership to innovate, to liberate. And at the zonal conferences, assembled for strategizing, "the Raders listened to every word, creating a sense of openness and giving people permission to explore different ways of evangelism."

People soon realized, Royston observed, that their recommendations offered at such conferences would not be forgotten. They discovered, doubtless to their pleasure and gratification, that upon the Raders' return to London their ideas would be considered. "They followed through." And out of these came the International Commission on Spiritual Life and the International Commission on Officership. From the commissions, in turn, according to Royston, came "recommendations that would turn some of our saints' hair gray overnight, but the Raders wanted to be down there in the groundswell so the Army could grow and change and move."

The standard against which the General and the World President of Women's Organizations measured all recommendations and action—their own as well as those taken by the Army—can be summed up in the answers to several basic questions: Why are we doing this? Does this benefit God's kingdom today? Will the Army grow because of this?

Along the way, as they grappled with the ideas and issues that affect the people and ministry for which they accepted responsibility, they acquired some honors that acknowledged their high-profile, innovative leadership of The Salvation Army. Honorary doctorates from Asbury College (LL.D.) for Paul, for both Paul and Kay from Asbury Theological Seminary (D.D.), Greenville College (L.H.D.), and Roberts Wesleyan College (D.D.), all in the United States, spoke of the recognition and respect they earned from Christian academia. And like a crown came the awarding of the GwangWha medal, The Order of Diplomatic Service, from Korea's President Kim DaeJung in a ceremony held in Seoul's Blue House and attended by two of their children, Edie and J. P., along with their spouses, all of whom reside in Korea. The citation reads, in part, "General Paul A. Rader, world leader of the Salvation Army, has rendered distinguished service in the field of mission to the Republic of Korea and the world . . . a great contribution to strengthening the welfare of the Korean people. His valuable dedication and service have earned for him the appreciation and admiration of the Korean people."

But when one attempts to talk about kudos and honors collected along their path, even the splendid gold and blue enamel medal from the Korean president, Paul Rader's eyes glaze over. His normally pungent, precise flow of descriptive rhetoric dries up, and someone else, if the conversation continues at all, must tell how it all happened and what it means.

Nudge Paul, however, to talk about their experiences across the world among the Army's missionary officers and the local Salvationist leaders and Christians who labor with them, to describe their efforts to share the name of Jesus among women and men unfamiliar with that name, and he lights up like New York's Time Square on New Year's Eve. Above all else, both Raders love to recount the "surprises" that ambushed them along the way, and their telling makes it sound as if they stood as mere observers at the results of someone else's labor.

On a ministry visit to Jos, Nigeria, capital of an African country dominated by Islam and therefore not at all receptive to Christianity, their expectations were not high. They moved into a rented hall only to find it packed with believers. Why were they there? To enroll no fewer than 80 new soldiers. "We were absolutely staggered!" Paul exults. "In Nigeria we met some of the most articulate lay spokespersons telling of their vision."

In Jessore, Bangladesh, a nation also Muslim and perhaps most famous for destructive monsoons, cyclones, and killer floods, the Raders were marched into a gathering of 3,000 Salvationists, the largest such Christian assembly ever held in that city. "It really took us by surprise!" Here Army workers "built something out of nothing, with floods and all that going on. They have this wonderful humanitarian work with prostitutes . . . a loan program . . . work with people with HIV and AIDS." They both glitter with excitement as they try to describe it.

Kay and Paul enjoy Africa and rejoice in the strong, well-ordered Army in Zimbabwe, "probably one of the best in Africa," they say. When they entered a large auditorium in Harare, part of a local hotel, for the Sunday morning meeting and saw the room and its balconies jammed with Salvationists in biscuit-colored uniforms and felt the energy exuded by such a crowd, "It took our breath away!" Paul says. Both he and Kay stood amazed by the crowd, touched by their singing and buoyed by their enthusiasm.

The Salvation Army's congress in Johannesburg, South Africa, culminated a year-long effort at reconciliation following that nation's jettisoning of apartheid, its system of racial separation. Paul was presented with a Book of Reconciliation that had traveled all over the country collecting signatures; he in turn passed it to the Black Chief Secretary for Southern Africa, Colonel William Mabena, for he knew it should not gather dust at International Headquarters in London, but remain in South Africa to remind all who saw it what had taken place.

From tables organizers made a huge cross that stood in the center of the auditorium, and people came to sign the covenant before this symbol of God's reconciling work of redemption. "To see these people come—Black, white, colored—all kneeling round the cross . . ." Paul begins to tell it and runs short of words. Kay picks up the thread. "We just wept."

Also in South Africa, the Raders visited the city of Soweto in an area set aside long ago for Black citizens. At the Sithole Center, named for a young Army officer who died there, they saw a babies' home, community center, and children's home and dedicated a monument bearing the words of the covenant.

"When we got done, one of the African officers started to sing and dance. Everyone joined in."

"What do the words mean?" Paul had to ask.

"It means it's all under the blood," he replied.

One wonders if that day Jesus saluted His followers at this, their moment of Christlike forgiveness.

Portuguese and Belgian gatherings Paul remembers as "not so large, but wonderful meetings." France, too, was small in number "but we had a marvelous time. The music and the spirit of the young people and their musical instruments were outstanding."

Mizoram, a state in northeast India, Paul describes as "tough to get to and to get out of, but when you're there, absolutely marvelous." The people reminded the Raders of Koreans with their Asiatic features and their enthusiasm for God. The Salvationists there call their corps "prayer halls," and as in Korea, music pervades the expression of their faith. Welsh missionaries taught these vigorous people to sing long ago and the memory of their lusty rendition of the "Hallelujah Chorus" still keeps both Rader hearts standing in worshipful attention.

So does remembering 20,000 Kenyan Christians, all in blinding white uniforms, marching under the scorching sun in their divisions by the General's reviewing stand. Being told that many of these people had already walked for hours just to be there, to be counted in the company of the redeemed, and to salute their international leaders brought a pair of hearts low before the Lord who made such a thing come to pass.

Small wonder that kudos, honors, and medals never assumed outsized proportions. Neither Paul nor Kay ever felt worthy to receive them. Kay, for her part, says they always meant "kindness and deference to the office of World President of Women's Organizations."

"Criticism sometimes is very hurtful, which comes with the territory," she continues. "Status quo leadership may be more comfortable; I don't know."

"One can be misunderstood, but by and large the majority were with us," Paul adds. "The highest kudos we got were letters from young people and officers who wanted us to know of God's call into officership. One such example: 'You give me new hope for the Army . . . new understanding of what my call is to be. Thank you for standing up for us.'"

"Leaders learn more than they teach," Kay reflects. "Every engagement we were involved with thrust us forward in the Spirit in a variety of ways. I thank the Lord for letting us be there when His wind was blowing over us."

"We never got over associating with people who were so committed to what God had called them to do, who fulfill their calling at great price, incredible loyalty, and devotion to God and those they serve," Paul says. "To have been leader to them is a remarkable privilege in the grace of God."

❊ ❊ ❊

"To have been leader to them," a phrase looking back on the past, sums it up well, because in July 1999 Paul and Kay Rader turned over Salvation Army leadership into the hands of John and Gisele Gowans and retired to their townhouse in Lexington, Kentucky. Their imprint remains on the Army God called them to serve. Evangelism, world missions, leadership development, and growth—spiritual and numerical—and a developing sensitivity to partnership within Army ranks and with other churches and agencies characterized their years at the helm. Willingness to change in concert with changing times is less terrifying to the average Salvationist than it used to be. An announcement by General Gowans in June 2000 informed the 25,000 people gathered in Atlanta in the United States for a centennial congress that Rader's Million Marching Campaign went over the top, that a million senior soldiers—1,019,137 to be exact—were enrolled from the 107 countries in which the Army labors.

Paul and Kay Rader are two Christians on the march, impelled, propelled by God, and capable of remarkable forward motion because they wrestled their way to the point of obedience to their Redeemer, to faithfulness to that hard-won commitment through the contrasts of bitter denial and overflowing abundance that marked their shared pathway.

And now, mature, seasoned, tempered, do they watch sunsets and reminisce? Maybe, at times. Do they plan frequent visits with children and grandchildren? Certainly. But there are also books to write, songs to sing, preaching requests to fulfill, children to smile at and listen to, a world full of people to love and learn about.

And yes, they have even more marches to lead, for when Asbury College's Board of Trustees, of which Paul is a member, quickly and unanimously in April 2000 appointed Paul to serve as the college's president upon David Gyertson's decision not to renew his contract, countless Rader friends, relatives, coworkers, colleagues, and fellow alumni approved with great joy.

In the months that followed, the search committee bent to their task of finding someone permanent. Then in March 2001 they brought their recommendation to the biannual meeting of the college board.

"Paul Rader should be our president."

In a second outpouring of enthusiasm and gratitude to God that Paul had agreed that his name be submitted for election to the presidency, board, faculty, students, and alumni celebrated the coming to pass of what many had wanted to see happen all along.

"Why look any further?" they had asked. "Can't Dr. Rader just keep on doing the job?"

Paul agreed to serve his alma mater, to guide the school where some of his most formative experiences took place, where he met and married Kay. And with that agreement, the Raders embarked on yet another mission, one woven into the seamless fabric of their partnership in ministry with each other and their Lord. God alone knows where this is leading and what else awaits, but as they stride along the path of His making, they agree to go . . . together.

If two of you shall agree on earth as touching any thing that they shall ask, it shall be done for them of my Father which is in heaven.

—*Jesus*
(Matt. 18:19, KJV)